Sacred
spaces

Sacred

spaces

creating
personal
altars and
shrines for
your home

josephine de winter

LORENZ BOOKS

This edition is published by Lorenz Books

Lorenz Books is an imprint of Anness Publishing Ltd
Hermes House, 88–89 Blackfriars Road, London SE1 8HA
tel. 020 7401 2077; fax 020 7633 9499
www.lorenzbooks.com
info@anness.com

© Anness Publishing Ltd 2002

Published in the USA by Lorenz Books, Anness Publishing Inc.
27 West 20th Street, New York, NY 10011; fax 212 807 6813

Published in Australia by Lorenz Books, Anness Publishing Pty Ltd
Level 1, Rugby House, 12 Mount Street, North Sydney, NSW 2060
tel. (02) 8920 8622; fax (02) 8920 8633

This edition distributed in the UK by Aurum Press Ltd
25 Bedford Avenue, London WC1B 3AT
tel. 020 7637 3225; fax 020 7580 2469

This edition distributed in the USA by National Book Network
4720 Boston Way, Lanham, MD 20706
tel. 301 459 3366; fax 301 459 1705; www.nbnbooks.com

This edition distributed in Canada by General Publishing
895 Don Mills Road, 400–402 Park Centre, Toronto,
Ontario M3C 1W3
tel. 416 445 3333; fax 416 445 5991; www.genpub.com

This edition distributed in New Zealand by David Bateman Ltd
30 Tarndale Grove, Off Bush Road, Albany, Auckland
tel. (09) 415 7664; fax (09) 415 8892

A CIP catalogue record for this book is available
from the British Library.

Publisher: Joanna Lorenz
Managing Editor: Helen Sudell
Senior Editor: Joanne Rippin
Photography: Michelle Garrett
Designer: Peter Clayman
Editorial Reader: Richard McGinlay
Production Controller: Claire Rae

10 9 8 7 6 5 4 3 2 1

This book is not intended to replace advice from a qualified
medical practitioner. Please seek a medical opinion if you have
any concerns about your health. Neither the author nor the
publishers can accept any liability for failure to follow this advice.

Contents

introduction

An altar is a meeting point, where the divine reaches down to touch the everyday world and where we can concentrate our intentions and desires for spiritual growth. There is a two-way flow between the individual and the world of spirit, and the altar is its channel. It can be both a setting for a journey into a spiritual dimension, and a place to gain deeper understanding of our own character and our place in the universe.

When you visualize an altar, you may imagine a monumental table in a lofty, echoing building, covered with a sumptuous cloth and with ritual objects formally arranged on it. Or perhaps you see an ancient monolith, open to the sky, potent with the memory of mysterious sacrifices and pagan rites. Altars like these are awesome and remote, approached only by priests and out of reach of ordinary worshippers. A different kind of altar – a simple shrine where you need no intermediary to help you reach the world of spirit – is the subject of this book. When you create a personal altar you place yourself at the very centre of your own sacred space, bringing the divine right into your life.

The domestic altar embodies the sanctity of home and family, and its presence helps to create a positive environment. It is a constant reminder of the search for spiritual fulfilment, anchored in the context of daily life. It can be a focus for prayer, a shrine to honour those you love, a place where you choose to meditate, or somewhere to spend a few minutes in quiet contemplation. The form it takes is up to you, but the themes and ideas explored in this book may help to inspire you as you begin to assemble your shrine. There are no rules to follow: all you need do is relax and enjoy the adventure of creation. In itself, the act of creating sacred space is a way of inviting spirit into your home and your life. It is like saying a prayer. Your altar will grow, change and develop as you do: take it with you on your spiritual journey.

Historical Perspective

The energy and potential of the altar has made it an important feature of sacred ceremony and ritual, wherever people gather to worship – in temples, churches or under the open sky.

Ancient shrines

A sense of the sacred pervades the history of humankind: all societies have shared an awareness of a greater power beyond the human, set apart from the normal routines of life. The earliest written records in the world are Sumerian, dating from about 3500 BC. In the references these contain to unseen beings and superhuman powers they clearly show the central importance of religion to those ancient people. But evidence of religious practice has also been found in the archaeological remains of earlier societies that far predated the written word.

Our earliest ancestors would not have tried to view themselves as separate from the natural world, as many people now prefer to do. They saw that they were part of the continuum of nature. Early humans were nomads, hunting and gathering food, and they were therefore dependent on their environment and perfectly integrated with it; their lives – like those of the animals they

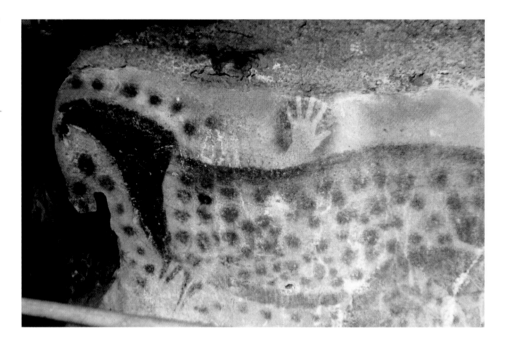

hunted – were regulated by the seasons. Recognizing their utter dependence on the earth, ancient people worshipped her as the universal deity. All aspects of the earth – rocks, trees, rivers, animals – shared her power and were seen as sacred: their energies, or spirits, were perceptible to the ancients in a way that our modern life generally obscures.

Appeasing the spirits

As nomadic societies settled down they developed tools, learned to harness the power of fire, raised domestic animals and practised agriculture. They began to gain some control over their environment, and their dependence on the natural world diminished as they learnt to grow and store food and build weatherproof shelters. Yet they continued to seek harmony in their own locality. As they felled trees for building materials, ploughed the soil, or took water from a stream or spring, they still felt the need to appease the earth spirits for the offences they felt they

△ Cave paintings, such as this speckled horse created c. 25,000 BC at Altamira in Spain, may be the oldest surviving evidence of shamanic ritual.

were committing against them. Sacrifices and offerings were made to ward off the ill-effects of these actions against nature.

Today, such traditions are still followed by people who preserve the animistic belief that everything in nature is infused with spirit. In western Alaska, for example, Yup'ik hunters believe that the spirits of the seals and walruses they catch are contained in the bladders of the animals, and these are preserved during the year. The Yup'ik hold an annual festival to propitiate the spirits. The event is preceded by a procession of boys from house to house, intended to open the whole community to the spirit world. An altar is set up and the bladders are inflated, painted and hung around it. Dried wild celery is burned and the smoke is used to purify both the bladders and the hunters. The fires are kept burning during singing, dancing and other rituals to propitiate the spirits and ensure good hunting for the following year. Then the bladders are carried to a hole in the ice, deflated and returned, with the spirits of the animals, to the sea.

△ The Sumerians left records of their religious ritual, such as this relief from c. 2500 BC showing the dedication of a chief to the god Ningirsu.

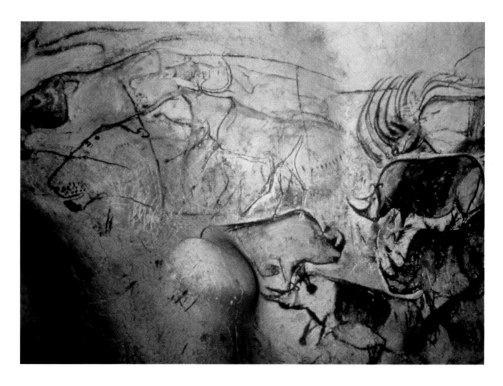

◁ Rhinoceroses, depicted in cave paintings dating from c.1800 BC, may represent powerful spirits with whom early shamans identified.

killed the monster Tiamat, who embodied the primeval salt-water ocean. In ritual, they symbolically re-enacted this event to affirm the banishing of chaos and the establishment of the ordered world.

Ritual is one explanation for numerous paintings of animals, created by palaeolithic hunter-gatherers and found on cave walls in

▽ Neolithic burial chambers built between 4500 and 2500 BC, such as this tomb at Locmariaquer, Brittany, were constructed to endure forever.

The role of ritual

For ancient people, sacrifice and ritual were attempts to placate, if not to control, forces that were potentially life-threatening. The world was a dangerous and unpredictable place in which existence was precarious, and the establishment of ritual represented one way in which humans could impose some order on their lives.

The recounting of myths was also a way of making sense of the world. Stories evolved in every society to account for the birth of humanity and the creation of our universe, and to give shape to the idea of continued existence after death in a parallel world of spirit. Many of the creation myths of early cultures presented cyclic visions of creation and destruction, with the world emerging out of chaos and eventually returning to it. This idea can be seen in the series of three worlds envisaged in the mythology of the native American Hopi people, the declining 'yugas' of Hinduism and the five ages of the ancient Greeks, beginning with the Golden Age and ending with the present Age of Iron.

The re-enactment of age-old rituals allowed the members of a culture to feel that they were participating in a larger reality beyond the limits of their own individual lives. The Mesopotamians, for example, believed that the world had come into being when Marduk, the supreme god,

France and Spain. The oldest of these have been dated to around 30,000 BC. Paintings of more recent date but which seem to have a similar purpose and significance have also been found in caves and rock shelters in Africa, Australasia and South America.

The artists who writhed their way deep into rock chambers to paint these images may have intended to animate and control the creatures they wanted to hunt, or – by depicting pregnant animals – to will their fertility and ensure a plentiful food supply. But while there are many depictions of bison, deer and horses, some of the oldest paintings, such as those at Chauvet in France, also feature rhinoceroses, lions, panthers and hyenas – dangerous animals that would not have been hunted for food. It is possible that the images are instead associated with shamanic ritual, and depict the shamans' identification with powerful animal spirits while in their trance state. The inaccessible caves and clefts where the paintings occur were seldom visited, and were perhaps known to only a few. They may have been viewed as meeting places between the human and the spirit worlds.

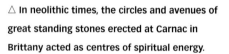

△ In neolithic times, the circles and avenues of great standing stones erected at Carnac in Brittany acted as centres of spiritual energy.

▽ The Aztec place of worship, called a *kiva*, was half submerged in the ground, symbolizing humanity's rootedness in the earth. Its focus was the central fire-pit, containing the fire of life.

Communicating with spirit

In animistic societies, shamans were important figures. They acted as intermediaries between the human world and the spirits of the earth. A shaman combined the roles of priest, healer and counsellor in the community, and his or her ability to communicate with spirits was a way of maintaining the wellbeing of the group – by ensuring a successful hunt, for instance, or predicting a drought. The shamans could enter a trance state in which they were freed from the normal human limitations of time, space and identity. They made journeys into the spirit world, often in animal form. They were set apart from ordinary people by their special powers and experience of other realities, and were treated with respect and awe.

One of the functions of the shaman was to act as guardian of a spiritual power that anthropologists now identify by a Polynesian word, *mana*. This supernatural power could exist in an object, such as a spear that had killed many animals or a lucky charm, and a person could gain power by touching such an object. (For some societies, words – above all, people's names – also possessed *mana*.) This idea of the sanctity of particular objects, which in due course came to include altars and shrines, led to the concept of a taboo, which forbade the touching of a sacred or powerful object, or the speaking of a particular word. Breaking a taboo could lead to punishment or even death, and only those with special dispensation – such as priests – would be permitted to approach sacred objects invested with *mana*.

△ **Native American shamans identified with powerful animal spirits by wearing their skins. By drumming and dancing to induce a trance state, they were able to enter the spirit world.**

Permanent altars

Places where earth energies were most powerfully felt by our ancient ancestors became sacred sites, where the people gathered to perform rituals and sacrifice offerings in order to give thanks, seek protection (from harmful influences) and gain the favour of spiritual powers. Throughout western Europe and Scandinavia, for instance, permanent structures began to be erected at special sites of worship from around 4800 BC. Many such shrines may have been constructed in earth or wood, but those that have endured were built using monumental stones, or megaliths. The oldest megaliths in the world are at Carnac in Brittany, where thousands of large stones are arranged to form avenues, chambers and mounds. Stone circles, of which the best known is Stonehenge in England, began to be constructed from around 3000 BC.

These mighty stone structures required huge resources of materials and manpower, and their survival demonstrates that those who built them certainly intended them to be permanent. They may have had astronomical as well as spiritual significance. They were perhaps attended by priests who could measure time, foretell eclipses and predict the movements of the stars. At Newgrange in Ireland, a prehistoric burial chamber is surrounded by a circle of twelve great stones. At the winter solstice, the rising sun shines directly into the passage to the chamber. The stones in the circle are aligned with sunrises and sunsets at the solstices and equinoxes, and are carved with symbols recording the movements of the sun, moon and planets.

The true purpose of Stonehenge is an enduring mystery, but its stones appear to be broadly oriented according to the direction of sunrise and moonrise at the solstices. Its circular form, echoing the larger circle of the horizon, has the effect of concentrating energy at its centre. It has recently been argued, for instance, that the inner surfaces of the standing stones were shaped in a very sophisticated way in order to amplify sounds – such as the prayers or chanting of a priest, perhaps – made within the circle. At the summer solstice, the sun rises over a single stone standing outside the circle, which is known as the heel stone. The heel stone casts its shadow over the central altar stone. While all the other stones of the monument are of sarsen or bluestone, the altar is a block of dressed green sandstone.

Stonehenge was constructed in various distinct phases over more than 1,500 years, and each phase added new elements to the site until the present arrangement was reached in about 1500 BC. Enclosed by concentric rings of stone, yet exposed to the sky and able to see the surrounding landscape through the stone screens, a participant in a ceremony at the monument's centre would have experienced a powerful connection with the natural world as the rising sun pierced the circle at the solstice.

▽ **Stonehenge, in Wiltshire, England, is one of the greatest megalithic monuments of Europe. The purpose for which it was built remains unknown, but modern visitors still sense its spiritual power.**

Altars of ancient civilizations

The earliest kinds of altars were open to the sky, with the smoke of burnt offerings rising towards the gods, but later they were enclosed in temples erected to honour specific deities. Like the hearth at the centre of the home, the altar was the focal point of a religious building, where ritual took place.

The house of the god

For the ancient Egyptians, a temple was not somewhere they congregated to worship a deity. No service was held there. It was literally the god's house, and very few were admitted to any part of it, least of all the innermost sanctuary where the god actually

△ The ancient Greeks sacrificed animals as burnt offerings on altars erected in the open air in front of the temples, so that the smoke from the fire could rise unhindered into the sky.

resided in the form of a cult statue. Ordinary worshippers came only to the outer precincts, to say prayers and leave votive offerings to enlist divine aid. To help the gods hear their prayers, the statues and walls were sometimes dotted with images of ears.

The Egyptians saw their deities in human terms, in need of family, food and shelter. Each morning, the high priest unsealed the shrine to tend the statue. Incense was burnt and a libation of water poured. The priest presented the god's breakfast as an offering, then brought out the statue to be cleaned and dressed in fresh linen and jewellery.

The hieroglyph for an offering – and for an altar – was a mat bearing a loaf of bread. The mat was later replaced by a stone table, grooved to receive libations of water, wine or milk and carved with images of food: magical substitutes for the real thing, to ensure that offerings would never cease.

◁ Detail from a sarcophagus, 16th century BC. The Egyptians used libations, or liquid offerings, to anoint and purify both deities and the dead.

Votive offerings

For the ancient Greeks, too, a temple was not a place for organized worship or private prayer. But they left votive offerings in return for a favour granted or as penance for a misdeed. These could be figurines, terracotta tablets, lamps, weapons or jewellery. At healing sanctuaries, replica body parts were sometimes offered in the hope of a cure. At major shrines such as Delphi, votive offerings could be elaborate monuments.

The Greek altar stood in front of the temple and was used to make burnt offerings of meat or fish. Grains, fruit, honey and incense were also offered. As the focus of public ceremony, altars in Ancient Greece became increasingly elaborate and important. Some stood alone, such as the vast altar of Zeus at Pergamum (now in modern Turkey), which had its own precinct but no temple. Built around 180 BC, the altar was decorated with a frieze of lifesize figures depicting the battle between the Olympian gods and the giants.

High altars such as this were dedicated to the gods, but both Greeks and Romans also honoured chehonian, or earth, deities, and their altars were constructed low in the earth: the Greeks poured libations into pits or trenches. Archaic altars were constructed from soil or stone to symbolize their connection with the earth.

Household gods

At home, the Greeks honoured Hermes and Hestia, the twin protectors of the house. A statue of Hermes, the god of transition and exchange, stood by the front door. Hestia presided over the hearth, representing stability and permanence. When a new baby was born, it was the tradition for Hestia's blessing to be sought by ritually carrying the child around the hearth.

The Romans, who borrowed many deities from the Greeks and other peoples they conquered, also worshipped the nameless spirits of the indigenous religion of Italy. These included the *lares*, ancestral spirits who protected the household. Figurines of the *lares* were kept in a special cupboard and the family made offerings to them every day, with more elaborate rituals on occasions such as weddings and birthdays.

The *penates* presided over the storeroom, and hence the family wealth. Their figurines were usually brought out to stand on the table during meals, and the family threw a portion of food into the fire as an offering to them. Another protective spirit, the household genius, took the form of a snake and presided over the marital bed: it was thought

▽ A *lararium*, the niche in which images of the *lares*, or household gods, were kept in a Roman home. Pompeii, 1st century AD.

to empower the fathering of children. The head of the family also made offerings to placate the spirits of the dead, who were known as the *lemures* and the *manes*. The god Janus guarded the door, and Vesta was the Roman goddess of the hearth. In her honour, the fire was kept burning constantly, day and night. Only if the family moved house was it extinguished, by pouring wine over it in a brief ritual.

Roman altars were short stone columns, with inscriptions carved on the side and an

△ Roman altars, such as this circular version, were designed for the purpose of making offerings, and were sometimes dedicated to 'all the gods in this place' to avoid offending a deity.

area known as the focus on top, where libations were poured or offerings of incense burned. Worshippers observed precisely defined rites; if a prayer or sacrifice was not performed absolutely correctly it was thought that the gods would be offended, and the ceremony had to be started again. For the Romans, correct procedure was the most important aspect of worship.

Eastern traditions

An enduring image of Eastern cultures is that of an altar shrouded in the smoke of incense sticks and sacred joss papers. The daily rituals of worship at altars in temples and homes have followed the same traditions for many centuries. As the great faiths of Hinduism, Buddhism and Islam arose and spread across Asia, each was adapted and absorbed by the indigenous cultures of the east, and the ancient rituals continued.

Vedic fire altars

The wisdom of Hinduism is contained in the four sacred texts called the Vedas. Begun during the second millennium BC, they predated the building of temples or the creation of holy images. Many of the deities invoked in the Vedic hymns, such as the storm god Indra and the sun god Surya, reflect aspects of nature. The ritual of ancient worship centred on the fire altar, and the presiding deity was Agni, the god of

▽ **Indra, the Hindu god of storms and war, portrayed here enthroned in his paradise, was revered as the leading deity in the Vedic period.**

fire. As sacrifices were offered in the fire, the flames and smoke rose to the gods, linking earth and sky. The daily fire worship was probably the most important aspect of religious observance.

The geometry of these early altars appears in appendices to the Vedas that set out the rules for their construction. The precise dimensions that were given varied for each year, because they were intended to reflect astronomical observations. Square altars were built to represent the sky while circular altars symbolized earth.

Because of the importance of the sacrificial fire, Agni came to be regarded as the mediator between humanity and the gods. Vedic hymns describe him as omnipresent – even in the rain, when he appears in the sky as lightning. It is Agni who devours the bodies of the dead on the funeral pyre. The fire altar is still important in Hindu worship, and is used in ceremonies such as weddings or the consecration of a new temple.

Buddhist veneration

The new philosophies of Buddhism and Jainism arose in India during the 6th century BC. By this time Hindus, like the

△ **Hindu priests prepare offerings of food at the Chettiar temple in Singapore.**

adherents of the new faiths, had begun to envisage human life as a cycle of birth and death, from which liberation had to be achieved. For Jains the path to enlightenment demanded physical austerities and mortification, following the example of the tirthankaras, or spiritual teachers. For Buddhists enlightenment was reached through inner struggle during meditation, aided by the example of buddhas and bodhisattvas who had already achieved it. Veneration of these exemplary figures helped people accustomed to worshipping deities to accept the new religion, and Buddhism flourished and spread widely.

Another Buddhist aid to meditation was the mandala, a kind of cosmic map representing the state of enlightenment. It could be a painting or a three-dimensional object, even a temple building. Tibetan monks today continue the tradition of creating a mandala in coloured sand, which is swept away at the end of the ritual. The map exists to be transformed into a sacred space in the course of contemplation.

Altar rituals in daily life

When Buddhism spread east from India, it blended with the older religions of China and other Far-Eastern cultures. The Chinese worshipped a complicated pantheon of Taoist gods and goddesses who inhabited a heaven modelled on the imperial court.

△ **A portable Japanese Buddhist shrine for use in personal devotions.**

Many household gods and spirits were honoured. There were guardian deities at the door, and a god that presided over each room, though it was most important to placate the kitchen god, Tsao-chun: each year he reported on the family's conduct to Yu Huang, the heavenly Jade Emperor. To ensure a good report, a farewell party was held for him with offerings of sweets, incense and paper horses.

In Japan, Buddhism mingled with the indigenous religion, Shinto. People continued to observe Shinto rituals of fertility, purification and rites of passage, while drawing on Buddhist philosophy when facing illness or seeking enlightenment and education. Religion remains part of the ordinary daily life of most Japanese people, and the household altar may be either a Shinto *kamidana* or a Buddhist *butsudan*, or ancestral altar.

The *kamidana* is a small altar enshrining protective deities, where offerings of food, water and flowers are regularly placed, and it is just as likely to be found in a shop or office as at home. The

Japanese regard the spirit world as very close, and call on gods for practical help in particular circumstances, such as passing an exam or having a baby. They may ask Jizo, protector of travellers, to bless a new car. He also protects children, and his statues are often hung with bibs belonging to the babies that he is asked to save. Kwannon, the goddess of compassion, has a special following among pregnant women and old people who want an easy old age.

Traditional Japanese houses have a special room set aside for the altar, though in smaller homes it simply occupies an elevated position. Another traditional feature is the *tokonoma*, an alcove in the north wall where scrolls are hung and flower arrangements or beautiful artefacts displayed. This, too, serves as a spiritual focus in the house.

The spirits of the ancestors

Veneration of the ancestors is an important tradition in the East. Their spirits have to be prevented from becoming restless or vengeful. Rituals ensure proper respect and provide the family with a means of consulting the wise elders, the family includes past and future generations as well as the present.

This continuity acts as a stabilizing influence in society. For Buddhists, veneration of the ancestors expands to include understanding of the connectedness of all things – everyone and everything ultimately has the same ancestors, so all are equally deserving of gratitude and love.

In the Chinese tradition, each person has two souls: the *hun*, or spiritual soul, goes to heaven, while the *p'o*, or physical soul, returns to the earth at death. The dead are therefore commemorated by two tablets: one for the *hun* on the altar in the family home and one for the *p'o* at the tomb. If the dead are properly interred with good feng shui and the correct sacrifices, they will use their spiritual power to confer blessings on the family. If neglected they will bring misfortune. Seeing that they are not neglected is the responsibility of the eldest son.

Many Japanese homes have a *butsudan*, a Buddhist altar enshrining the ancestors. Among the candles, statues and incense, the tablet of each ancestor bears his or her *kaimyo*, the new spirit name given after death. Families use the altar to talk to the ancestors, relaying family news, and children may have to apologize to the ancestors if they are naughty. Even those with no religious belief take part in these family rites.

△ A festival altar piled with offerings of fruit and other food to welcome the ancestors home.

▽ **In Penang, Malaysia, a Chinese woman leaves offerings by the door, inviting her late husband's spirit back into the house.**

Imperial Chinese altars

At the beginning of China's history in the second millennium BC, ancestor worship lay at the heart of state religious practice. The supreme god Shang Ti was worshipped as the ancestor of the founding Shang dynasty. Subsequent dynasties also venerated Shang Ti, and each built an Altar of Heaven to the south of its chosen capital city.

The altar was a three-tiered circular platform, full of numerical symbolism based on the yang or heavenly numbers (9, 5 and 3) and the cosmic numbers 72, 108 and 360. It was used for the great imperial sacrifice made at dawn on the winter solstice. After three days of fasting and meditation, the emperor, facing north, made offerings to Shang Ti and the deities of the sun, moon, stars, clouds, rain, wind and thunder. In 1530 the Ming dynasty erected an Altar of Earth to the north of Beijing as a counterpart to

the Altar of Heaven. A two-tiered square structure surrounded by a moat, it used the symbolism of yin or earthly numbers (6, 8 and their multiples). At the summer solstice, with perfect symmetry, the emperor, facing south, worshipped the earth and the spirits of the four seas, the four rivers and the four sacred mountains.

Feng shui

Chinese altars, like all other buildings, were positioned following the precepts of feng shui, the ancient art of placement. For centuries, the principles of feng shui were transmitted orally or through poetry and paintings, though a text from the Han Dynasty (206 BC–AD 220) describes how it was applied to the siting of the Chinese emperors' tombs. The Form School of feng

△ A small Shinto shrine in Fukushima, Japan, typically situated in a natural wooded setting.

19

historical perspective

shui was founded in the 9th century AD. It assessed a site visually, considering the flow of *chi*, or energy, the balance of yin and yang (negative and positive forces), the influence of the four directions and the form a building should take to ensure the harmony of the five elements (see box).

An ideal location would have had an open space in front, perhaps with a pool or meandering stream, and protective hills behind. If there was a prominent hill to the left it would be identified symbolically as a dragon, which would bring good fortune to those living in the place. In a city, the flow of the river could be imitated by traffic in the street, and the place of hills and mountains would be taken by surrounding buildings. If the location was less than ideal, the garden provided opportunities for introducing elements to balance the existing landscape.

THE FOUR SYMBOLIC ANIMALS

The four directions are symbolized by animals, and they are also used to describe the sides of a building, regardless of compass direction.
RED PHOENIX: the south or front; summer, fame, fortune, optimism.
BLACK TORTOISE: the north or back; winter, the family, relaxation.
GREEN DRAGON: the east or left side (looking out of the door); spring, health and protection, kindness, wisdom, growth.
WHITE TIGER: the west or right side; autumn, anger, sudden movement.
If the unpredictable tiger is too weak, life can be boring, but if he is not kept in check by the dragon, he can prove dangerous.

▽ The circular Altar of Heaven, Beijing, where the emperor officiated at the winter sacrifice to the heavenly deities of the sun, moon and stars.

THE HARMONY OF THE ELEMENTS

The interaction of the five Chinese elements is the basis of feng shui:
WOOD: east, plant life, green, tall, narrow shapes.
FIRE: south, the sun, animal life, red, triangular shapes.
EARTH: the centre, earth and earthen materials, ochre, flat shapes.
METAL: west, autumn, silvery white, metal implements, circular shapes.
WATER: north, fluidity, communication, darkness, irregular shapes.
If one element dominates a location, it will affect human and natural events: to avoid adverse effects, it can be balanced by introducing other features.

The elements influence each other in a natural productive cycle. Following this leads to harmony, health and prosperity: WOOD fuels FIRE which produces ash, or EARTH, the source of METAL, which melts into WATER, which nourishes plants to produce WOOD.

There is also a destructive cycle, which is also natural but may interfere with harmonious living if it is not neutralized: Wood takes nourishment from Earth which absorbs Water which extinguishes Fire which melts Metal which cuts Wood.

Feng shui practitioners of the more formal Compass School used a very complex compass called the *lo pan* to assess the flow of *chi* and particularly to decide on the best internal layout of a building. The *pa gua* is an element of the *lo pan* which is now often used separately in popular adaptations of feng shui to work out the best arrangements of rooms within a house, and the furniture in it – including altars.

Altars in temples and churches

As the place of offering and communication with the divine, the altar is still the centre of action in many of the world's established religions. It is the place where oaths are sworn, marriages solemnized and blessings bestowed. The idea of offering or sacrifice is common to all religions and the altar is the structure on which offerings – whether actual or symbolic – are made.

Making offerings

In Hindu belief, the altar, or offering place, is the metaphorical centre of the world, and a temple built around it is the home of the gods. The ritual of worship, called *puja*, is intended to attract their attention. The intangible deities become accessible through their images on the altar and the rituals of devotion. These rituals are designed to focus all five senses of the worshippers as they wash the statues of the gods and anoint them with perfumed oils, offer food and flowers, burn incense and ring bells. The

▽ The Buddhist altar is a place of meditation, inspired by the serene image of the Buddha himself or another spiritual master.

△ A 19th-century image of the Hindu goddess Kali on a simple altar in a Thugee temple.

prominent eyes of the statues are designed to help the worshippers make visual contact with the divine.

The gods are also worshipped at home, since the ritual is an individual act and the offerings are personal ones, though family members worship together. At home the shrine is usually a small altar, though it could be a whole room or just a picture or statue. An oil lamp invokes Agni, the fire god, and incense is waved before the deities' images.

Buddhist veneration

In a Buddhist home, monastery or temple, the altar creates a sacred space for meditation. Its three elements – a *sutra* (scripture), a statue and a *stupa* (domed shrine) – symbolize the Buddha's perfected speech, body and mind. The long ears of the Buddha signify his wisdom, and his topknot represents the higher consciousness. The statue is usually of the Buddha but it could be of Chenrezig, Tara, Manjushri or another spiritual master. On a small, personal shrine, the statue may be hollow so that mantras can be written and placed inside to bless it. Offerings are

made each morning of flowers, food, fragrance, water for drinking and for washing, incense, music (a conch shell or bell) and light (butter lamps or candles). The offerings traditionally go in seven matching bowls, placed side by side almost touching to symbolize closeness to the Buddha.

Church altars

Many different styles of altar are found in churches today, depending on the denomination of the worshippers and the age of the building. The development of the altar reflects the history of Christian thought.

For Christians the idea of sacrifice is specifically associated with the crucifixion, rather than with offerings made on an altar. But the cult of martyrs led to an association of altars with relics. Masses were often held on tombs to honour the dead and obtain their intercession, and many churches were built over the tombs of martyrs. Where this was impossible, the relics were brought to

▽ An elaborate Baroque high altar of the early 18th century in the Cloister Church of Fürstenfeldbruck, Germany.

◁ **Water from a holy well flows under this stone altar in St Cledarus' Chapel, Cornwall, England.**

bring in the sabbath light, and the father recites blessings over the wine and bread, elevating the physical act of eating and drinking into a spiritual dimension.

Sacred space

There are no altars in Islam. The holiest shrine of Muslims is the Ka'aba in Mecca, the site of God's first house on earth established by Abraham, and in prayer the faithful turn to face it. A niche in the mosque wall, called the *mihrab*, indicates the direction, and is the most sacred part of the building. The faithful repeat prayers five times a day, and though they are said to be more meritorious when recited in the mosque, they can be said anywhere: outside the mosque, a prayer rug forms the sacred space required.

▽ **Bread and wine – Jewish symbols of light and life – ready for the family sabbath meal.**

the churches, and altars took the form of boxes to contain them.

In the Middle Ages, the practice of saying private masses meant that some cathedrals in western Europe contained dozens of altars in addition to the 'high' altar. Having begun in the middle of the church, this gradually moved back to the apse wall. The growing distance between the congregation and the altar was underlined by the addition of a rood screen, and the altar was increasingly obscured by steps, candles, flowers, statues and curtained canopies.

Protestants rejected the connection between the altar and sacrifice by using a movable table, placed away from the apse wall in the midst of the congregation. The reformers stripped away the screens that made the altar distant and mysterious. In the century following the Reformation in England, communion tables were placed so that the communicants could gather around them to share symbolically the bread and wine of the Last Supper.

Worship without an altar

The Old Testament describes the tabernacle carried by the Jews during their wanderings in the wilderness. As they were on the move, their sacred shrine had to be in the form of a portable tent which was constantly being dismantled and reassembled. Ritual evolved to ensure that the altar, candles and incense were assembled correctly.

The courtyard of Solomon's Temple in Jerusalem contained a sacrificial altar, at which burnt offerings were made morning and evening, with additional offerings on the sabbath. But after the destruction of the Temple, the Jews decreed that their altar could stand nowhere else: the sacrificial system was replaced by prayer, with specific services standing for the morning and evening sacrifices, and special prayers for the additional offerings. The family table has taken the altar's place in Jewish domestic ritual. Each sabbath begins with a special meal on Friday evening that is shared by the whole family. The mother lights candles to

Altars in the new age

Connecting with the sacred seems to be a universal human need, which often remains strong even in those who find it hard to relate to the conventions of established religions. In the present secular age many people still seek the security of the spiritual, especially at times when the world seems chaotic and frightening. Some look to new religious groups, while others adopt versions of ancient traditions.

There is a growing sense in the Western world that modern life in our fast-paced, industrialized society has led to a loss of contact with our roots in nature. The trend towards the revival of the old pagan practices can be seen as an attempt to restore these links and reconnect humanity with the rest of the universe.

Following shamanic tradition

Those skilled in the practices of the old life-affirming faiths, such as native American shamans, preserve traditions of worship that can help us to honour and co-operate with

▽ Statues or images of the Goddess are frequently placed on pagan altars.

△ A native American altar rock in New Mexico, inscribed with nature symbols.

nature. We may no longer be able to live a life that is perfectly integrated with the natural world, but we can learn from them ways of focusing our intent to celebrate life rather than destroy it.

The wheel is an archetypal emblem that features in many of the faith systems of the world. In the native American tradition it appears as the medicine wheel, also known as the sacred hoop, and is an important symbol of spiritual belief. It represents the cycles of life – illustrating the relentless progress of birth, death and rebirth, as well as the annual succession of the seasons – and points to the way in which nothing really ends or disappears, but is transmuted into new forms. Like the Buddhist mandala, the medicine wheel offers a guide to enlightenment through contemplation.

In the shamanic tradition, an altar – which could be a cairn, a stone circle, or simply a flat piece of rock or wood – serves as a focus of the energy of spirit. It is a place to leave offerings to honour the connectedness of the universe. The offerings are usually natural, such as salt or tobacco.

▷ Shamanic rituals include simple offerings of salt or tobacco, and use natural elements.

Neo-pagan worship and ritual

Pagan beliefs are rooted in the ancient traditions of nature religions, which regarded deities as embodiments of aspects of the natural world. The traditions of neo-paganism are vibrant and changing, but many are based on Celtic and pre-Celtic practices, with festivals celebrating the seasons.

△ **In Glastonbury, Somerset, a notable centre for pagan thought, this altar was created on the occasion of a conference on the Goddess.**

The neo-pagan tradition of Wicca honours the sanctity of the earth through song, dance, invocation and ritual. Many Wiccans also cast spells for healing, happiness and empowerment. The Wiccan altar provides a focal point for ceremonies, and a place where the working tools of ritual are empowered. Ritual charges the altar with energy and it is approached with respect.

Rather than the patriarchal emphasis of established religions, neo-pagans recognize the concept of the Goddess and God as dual expressions of the divine. The Goddess has a central role in modern spirituality. As Mother Earth, she was worshipped by ancient peoples as the giver of all life and fertility. The rise of feminist awareness in the West has led to a reappraisal of male-dominated religion and the way in which it suppressed the earth-centred, intuitive, generative power of the female principle. When female divinities have been placed in the heavenly hierarchy, it is always in a lower position than a male creator god, but they have often provided a more personal, approachable face of the divine, and access to it. Female deities' shrines are usually the most visited, and inspire the greatest adoration.

THE CELTIC YEAR

Many modern pagan practices are based on the Celtic tradition, in which eight major seasonal festivals are celebrated. Together they make up the 'Wheel of the Year', whose name reflects the Celtic understanding of natural cycles of growth, decay and rebirth. The Wheel incorporates the solar festivals of the solstices and equinoxes, alternating with four festivals that mark important dates in the traditional farming year, and therefore connect with nature and earth energies.

IMBOLC 1–2 Feb
Return of the light. The beginning of the lambing season, and the first milk of the year
OSTARA (Spring Equinox)
21 or 22 March
BELTANE 30 April – 1 May
May Day: the coming of summer, when cattle were driven outside into the fields.
SUMMER SOLSTICE 21 or 22 June
LUGHNASADH 31 July – 1 August
Feast of Lugh, god of light. The major cattle fair of the summer, and harvest festival.
AUTUMN EQUINOX
21 or 22 September
SAMHAIN 31 October – 2 November
The end of summer, when cattle were brought inside for the winter or slaughtered for meat.
WINTER SOLSTICE
21 or 22 December

The Goddess has many aspects. Examples of her complex nature can be found in the three faces of the Triple Goddess – maiden, mother and crone – and the dual aspect of the Hindu Shakti, who is both Parvati, the gentle mother, and Kali, the avenger. Goddesses of the Egyptian, Greek and Celtic pantheons are being rediscovered and honoured today because the many qualities they hold help to redefine the feminine as creative, affirming and powerful.

Altars and shrines in nature

The pressures of modern life make it easy to feel disconnected and isolated. When we need to be reminded that life is a precious gift, the natural world is the best place to find tranquillity and inspiration. When we seek the restorative power of nature, the energy of growing plants and rushing water, the movement of the breeze and the good smell of fertile soil slowly infuse our being, bringing renewed vitality and clearer thoughts.

At sites where the positive energy of the earth is most powerfully felt, people have always performed rites and ceremonies to

▽ **In a ruined chapel in the Scottish Highlands, this altar has survived and is now imbued with the energy of its natural surroundings.**

honour the spirit of the place. In ancient times, rites of earth worship would have been attached to the times of year when the spirits were most active and their help most needed. A sacrifice to the spirit of the local stream, for example, would have been made to safeguard the water supply in summer.

Holy springs

Springs, where fresh water bubbles naturally out of the earth, are life-giving and earth-given, and are held in special reverence in many cultures. Water flowing underground carries strong earth energy, which can be detected by dowsing. A natural spring, the point where the water forces its way out of the earth, is therefore a powerful focus for

energy. In many places, old beliefs tell that drinking from or bathing in a particular spring or well can help to promote fertility or cure illness.

In Europe, as the Church absorbed old sacred places, many wells were given the names of Christian saints to obscure their origins in earlier nature religion, but the spiritual power of the shrines was still acknowledged. The custom of leaving offerings for the spirit of a spring is still widely observed: annual ceremonies of well-dressing with flowers still take place in several parts of Britain and Ireland, and most people at some time have tossed a coin into a well or pool while making a wish.

Trees of power

Large trees are also powerful landmarks, significant witnesses to the spirit of the earth. In an arid land, they indicate the presence of water and life, so they have often been honoured as fertility symbols and associated with fertility rites – 'marriage oaks' were once common.

The size of a mature tree dwarfs humans and its life can span many human generations, reminding us of the continuity of nature. A great tree, with its roots locked deep into the earth and its branches reaching up into the sky, helps us to appreciate the connectedness of creation. The image of the tree of knowledge occurs in the mythologies of many cultures, such as Yggdrasil, the Norse world tree, or the holy trees growing on the Japanese Mountain of Heaven. Sacred groves of trees were ancient sites of worship and divination, and aspects of tree magic lie behind modern customs such as bringing in evergreens at Christmas.

Eternal stones

Just as huge trees have the power to alter our perception of ourselves, rocks, hills and mountains convey the immensity and age of the natural world. Climbing a hill can be a trial of endurance: the physical effects, as

▷ This beautiful open-air altar has been made from a simple pile of natural Welsh slate.

▽ An ancient tree, left standing where it grew, is carved to represent the spirit of the wood.

well as the fresh view of the world from the summit, may result in new insights and increased perceptions. Inaccessible mountains were once thought to be the homes of the gods, and holy hills dot the landscape. Stones from heaven – meteorites – have traditionally been especially revered, and have formed the centre of important religious shrines, such as the Ka'aba in Mecca and the original Omphalos at Delphi.

Making a personal natural altar

Most people have a particular place that they visit when they need time alone, to meditate or just to relax. Such a place could be a part of a garden, a particular tree or a rock on a hill. Like the traditional holy sites, these places have a natural power, but they also take on the energy of those who visit them: they become sacred space.

Some people feel drawn to traditional natural shrines, while others seek a place that is uniquely special to them, such as a beautiful meadow or an ancient fallen tree in a glade. It will be somewhere that inspires a feeling of being part of creation, a place

where we are able to meditate on the complexity of nature, feel its vitality and reflect on our part in the immensity of the universe. As we use all our senses to appreciate the beauty of the surroundings, the feeling of connection grows stronger.

A flat rock or a tree stump can often resemble an altar, or a sacred space can be created by forming a circle with stones, twigs or cones, though nothing should be added or changed in a way that disturbs the natural harmony of the place. Leaving a small offering on a natural shrine is a way of expressing gratitude for the feeling of oneness with nature that it has inspired, helping to formalize and sanctify the experience.

▷ Prehistoric stone circles, such as the Ring of Brodgar on Orkney, are so rooted in the landscape that they seem almost part of nature.

Altars Through Life

A sacred space brings positive energy into your home and life. Your altar and the precious objects you place on it will help to focus that energy.

A personal altar

It is in times of solitude and quiet reflection that we find the space we need to centre and renew ourselves, and to gain the patience and wisdom it takes to deal with all that life throws at us. We need time to see beyond the mundane and the everyday, to find a way of viewing life as a connected whole, and to feel integrated with that whole: to achieve a sense of spirit.

Creating a personal altar is a way of inviting spirit into your home. The sacred space it occupies is available to you all the time, whenever you need an interval of repose to nourish your soul and restore your sense of the sacred. As you use your altar for prayer or meditation you energize it, and its influence widens, flowing out through and around you, to sanctify your home and everyone in it. An altar can be a physical expression of your deepest attachments and longings; by giving them form you bring them into your daily life and empower yourself to achieve what you desire.

△ **We instinctively bestow significance and importance on items of remembrance, and make out of them tiny, temporary shrines.**

Instinctive altars

Most of us display an instinctive need to enshrine what is precious to us. If you look around your home you can probably already find an altar you have created unconsciously – perhaps several. The lovely sea shells you collected during last summer's holiday, the family photographs upon the mantelpiece, the candles and flowers in the centre of the table: we all make such arrangements with love and care, and they inspire us with feelings of harmony and beauty.

Young children naturally make altars of their favourite toys. They will often arrange their most special things so that they can look at them as they go to sleep and find them still there when they wake in the morning. If a child is sick or upset, arranging some pretty things on her bedside table will help to cheer her up. Children have a wonderful ability to invest all kinds of objects with magic. A child will turn a handful of toffee wrappers into jewel-

△ **A simple altar for a child that is a collection of their favourite things, will encourage them to build a magical relationship with their spirit.**

coloured windows, transforming his familiar surroundings. Fragments of translucent, sea-worn glass, with their delicate colours and subtle texture, are valued as rare marine gemstones. Leaf skeletons or unusual feathers picked up in the park are mysterious treasures – the fresh vision of children can teach us to see such things as they really are: small miracles of natural form.

As children grow up they need to establish their separate identity and personal space. The teenager's room is a shrine to growing individualism (which may mean that it's a mess). Friendships might be celebrated by a whole wall full of photographs, reinforcing the good feeling of being a member of a supportive group. Another wall might be devoted to posters of pop stars, but there may still be a shelf somewhere

29

◁ Setting aside an area of a room purely for reflection, prayer or meditation will help to bring a spiritual element into your life.

with just a few flowers and a single candle, and you can add items as they become significant. It will evolve as you use it and your relationship with it grows closer and stronger, until all its various elements mirror the many facets of your personality.

Practical considerations

Any flat surface can become an altar when it is hallowed by intent. It needs to be somewhere quiet, where no one will bump into it as they pass and where you will be able to stand, sit or kneel before it comfortably. But if it suits you, the surface could be a shelf, a windowsill with a tranquil view beyond, the top of a chest, even the top of the refrigerator.

Traditionally, altars have been made from natural materials, often wood. If you choose to make a shrine on an old piece of furniture, it will hold the resonance of its past use, while a new piece could be the foundation of an altar for new beginnings. Prepare the space the altar will occupy by removing clutter from the surrounding area and cleaning everything until it sparkles.

△ A bowl of floating candles, lit to create a welcoming atmosphere for visitors, is one of the simplest altars.

dedicated to some much-loved toys, whose missing eyes and worn fur show how much emotion was invested in them – a little altar to the childhood that is being left behind.

Creating an altar with intent

The altar is a work of intuition and imagination. As you play around with ideas for it, handling and thinking about the objects you are placing on it, you will be feeding into it your own energy and creativity, making it more deeply personal. You will know instinctively when it is right. Allow your

creativity to flow freely, straight from your spirit. The intention behind what you place on an altar, and what it represents, is more important than its physical reality.

Your altar can be for you alone, or to share with others. A family altar can work for cohesiveness, like the traditional ancestral altars of the East. A couple could share in the creation of an altar to promote a deeper commitment to one another.

Let your altar grow freely, moving things around, or setting up a new altar whenever you wish. It can begin very simply, perhaps

Altars through the home

Most people have one room that feels special, where the sense of positive energy is most complete. It could be the living room, the kitchen, or a welcoming entrance hall. Traditionally, the hearth is regarded as the centre of the home and is really a prototype altar. But if you want an altar to be very personal to you, you may prefer to have it in a more private place.

Feng shui can help you position your altar effectively, using the directional chart called the *pa gua* to find areas that represent the various aspects of your life. An altar in the wisdom and experience area could benefit your spiritual life, while an altar dedicated to love would be most effective in the relationships area. The *pa gua* can also be imposed on a room to determine the best placement for an altar, or on the altar itself to help you arrange objects on it.

All the different activities that we pursue create distinct types of energy in each room. This is why it can be very difficult to get to sleep in a room that has been full of lively conversation, for instance, or to concentrate on a piece of analytical work in the kitchen. Every altar will be influenced by the energy of its surroundings. You can use this power to create a life-enhancing altar

◁ **This simple bedroom altar to Gaia, the goddess of dreams, includes lillies to invoke calm.**

in any room by drawing on the intrinsic energy of the space, and there is no reason why you shouldn't have several small altars around the house, wherever you feel they are needed.

The bedroom

Most of us want our bedroom to be a sanctuary where we can be wholly ourselves. It is where we take our secrets and prayers, joy and grief. A bedroom altar acts as a focus for these, and for daily rituals to help you greet the day and prepare for night.

△ **A bedroom altar reminds us as we wake that the spirit of the sacred is always with us.**

For peaceful rest, place sleep crystals on your altar: amethysts, a piece of jade or obsidian. The scent of lavender or jasmine will help you sleep. Honour the earth deity and goddess of dreams, Gaia, with barley grains or laurel, or include an image of Nephthys, who sheltered the sleeping pharaohs beneath her protective wings.

At bedtime, set a bowl of water scented with jasmine oil near your bed and place your sleep crystals in it. On willow leaves – to help your wishes come true – write what you wish to come to you in sleep.

▷ Our working environment, like any other, benefits from a spiritual atmosphere. An office altar dedicated to Thoth encourages inspiration.

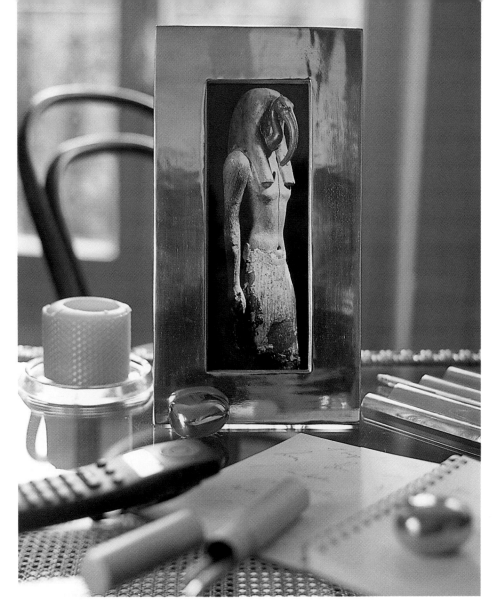

THE FOUR DIRECTIONS

Ancient traditions honour the four directions of the compass, and attribute specific qualities to each one. The custom is preserved in the architecture of Christian churches and Buddhist temples, where the altar always stands in the east. By placing an altar in a particular direction, you can harness its particular qualities.

EAST: new beginning and rebirth.

SOUTH: motivation, creativity and growth.

WEST: healing and transformation.

NORTH: looking within.

There is, however, a Buddhist saying, 'Where faces the yogi, there is the east of the yogi': in other words, 'the east within' – your own state of mind – is more important than geographical direction.

The study or office

An altar in the workplace will generate positive energy to help you concentrate. Wisdom and inspiration are personified by Thoth, the scribe of the Egyptian gods who wrote down the wisdom of the universe.

Yellow candles assist communication and learning. Helpful crystals include emerald, to give insight, azurite, for clarity, and hematite, to aid reasoning and memory.

The hallway

The Roman god Janus is a traditional protective deity, and could stand on a shrine by the door, or it could house a guardian animal such as a dog, lion or tiger. Sacred objects at the entrance help to sanctify the whole of your home, and you will carry blessings with you as you leave.

The kitchen

At the hub of the house, the kitchen is a potent place. The energy of the earth – in the form of food – is transformed by the magical process of cooking, which demands creativity and concentration. An altar for

◁ A kitchen altar can incorporate any kind of food, although traditionally it would have included grains, honey and spices.

hospitality could be dedicated to Hestia, goddess of the hearth and home, or to Demeter, goddess of abundance and unconditional love. Leave offerings of rice, grains, fruit or honey for the nature spirits and light the altar candles each time you prepare a meal. A shrine behind the sink would engage your attention as you work there. You could hang herbs and flowers, chilli and garlic around the window like a garland, or decorate the sill with evergreens.

The living room

To promote harmony between your family and friends, set up an altar to the four elements on the mantelpiece. This could combine salt for earth, a red candle for fire, sea shells for water and feathers for air.

Green is the colour of harmonious relationships. To create a prayer bowl, place a clear quartz cluster in a green bowl full of spring water and invite members of the family to write down their prayers for others and tuck them under the bowl.

Collecting natural offerings

We are part of the natural world, even if urban living makes us feel removed from it. We rely on nature for food and sustenance, and have a responsibility as its caretakers. Placing natural objects on an altar helps to reinforce its connection with earth energies, and underlines our commitment to preserving the natural world.

Nearly everyone has at some time brought home a beautiful stone or sea shell as a souvenir of a precious day, or because it came from a place that made us feel happy, somewhere we felt a sense of spiritual peace. The resonance of that experience clings to the object for ever. In school, the tradition of maintaining a nature table encourages children to share their unusual and beautiful natural finds with others. This kind of display also involves a kind of reverence for the wonders of the earth, and can become a visual calendar, recording the cycle of the seasons.

Reverence for nature of course precludes stealing from it: if you are moved by a beautiful natural environment, the last thing you want to do is disturb it. Rather than cutting flowers or trees, you may prefer to take only things that have fallen. Leave an offering to signify your appreciation of the gift. This could be a traditional offering, such as

▽ **Fossils represent the ancestors and past life memory. Placing a fossil on an altar will aid memory and help us find our roots.**

tobacco – which is considered a sacred herb by native Americans – or salt, sacred to the Celts. Or express your gratitude in a simple action, such as clearing away litter.

Flowers and trees

Plants are great healers, both physically and spiritually. If you respond particularly strongly to a flower or tree, keep it or an image of it on your altar. Trees are powerful emblems of nature, and each has its special attributes and symbolism.

According to legend, the birth of Gautama Buddha was greeted with birdsong and showers of sweet tea and fragrant flowers, and this is why fresh flowers are placed on Buddhist altars. Flowers are a universal symbol of youth and gentleness, and an appreciation of their beauty has helped civilizations to flourish artistically since

△ **Driftwood carried by the oceans conveys the blessings of the Goddess and can be placed on an altar dedicated to emotional healing.**

▽ **Flowers are filled with grace and beauty, and can remind us of our own innate qualities of innocence and purity.**

▷ Pebbles and stones represent the earth element. Their presence on an altar can help to stabilize stress-filled atmospheres.

TREE ASSOCIATIONS
APPLE: youth, beauty, innocence.
ASH: the world tree, purification and cleansing.
BAY: guardian of the house, protection against illness.
BEECH: stability, flow of energy, protector of knowledge.
DOGWOOD: charm and finesse.
HAWTHORN: marriage, fertility, protection of children.
HAZEL: wisdom and fertility, used to divine water.
OAK: wisdom, strength and endurance.
ROWAN: protection against evil.
WILLOW: love and regeneration, lunar and feminine rhythms.
YEW: immortality, transformation and inner wisdom.

cleanse and protect the house. They can be placed on an altar to represent particular qualities. Basil, for example, is said to protect from pain, and sage is a purifying herb.

Fruits, nuts and grains
At harvest time, it is traditional to bring offerings of nuts, fruit and grain to the altar to give thanks for the abundance of nature. The fruits brought for blessing contain within them the seeds of next year's crop, so this ritual of thanksgiving also includes a prayer for fertility in the future.

Stones and sea shells
A stone belongs to the earth and brings grounding energy to the altar. It conveys the character of the place where it originated: the moving river bed, the windswept seashore or the eternal mountains. Rocks and stones also carry the resonance of millions of years of history, and fossils remind us even more vividly of the antiquity of earth's life story, of which we are a part.

Emblems of the sea, shells are associated with its fluid, feminine energy. They signify water, the element of the emotions. They also have traditional links with regeneration, baptism and prosperity.

Feathers
Representing the element of air, feathers symbolize the connection between earth and heaven, and therefore between humanity and the creator. Their complex structures and natural beauty make them valuable objects for contemplation during meditation.

▽ Feathers represent birds, who are honoured as a link between earth and heaven.

ancient times. Their brief lives encapsulate the cycle of birth, life and return to the earth to nurture the next generation. A single flower is an expression of natural but fleeting perfection. Gazing into it, you can find peace and serenity that you can take into yourself.

Herbs
The use of herbs – for healing, spiritual cleansing and magic – has a long history. Many are tried and tested remedies, and almost every plant is useful in some way.

Herbs are used as talismans in magic: St John's wort, for example, is hung over windows and doors on Midsummer's Day to

Objects of beauty

While you are assembling your altar, it will help you to decide on the form it is to take if you constantly keep in mind your purpose and intention: that you are honouring the spiritual centre of your life and providing a focus for it. All the elements you bring to the altar, such as candles, incense, pictures and objects that are important to you, are tools to help you to this end. Make your altar beautiful, so that each time you see it, it lifts your heart.

Sacred images

Deities from any religion may have a personal symbolism for you, whether or not you are an adherent of any faith. A statue of the Buddha in meditation could help with your own meditation and prayer, for example, while a picture or statue of St Francis of Assisi may have special meaning if you have a deep affinity with animals.

In the Christian church, the symbolic power of imagery is seen in the icon, a visual expression of faith. The Byzantine artists of the early Church developed a characteristic style for the painting of these holy pictures, using a language of symbols to transmit the tenets of Christianity to worshippers who could not read the scriptures for themselves. Because God had appeared on earth in human form, it was felt that the image of the human Christ could be por-

▽ Statues of female or male figures will honour the archetype you wish to represent.

trayed to help the faithful understand the nature and intention of God.

Icons can be anything from small paintings on wood panels or paper, to large frescoes. Their nature is defined not by their size but by their sacred subject matter and the traditional style and symbolism used to depict its essence. They are recognized universally as objects of great beauty and power. In the West, they tend to be regarded as symbols of faith, comparable with a cruci-

△ Creating an altar with objects of personal meaning can reinforce spiritual connections.

fix or a stained glass window. In the mystical tradition of the Orthodox church, however, they are precious objects of prayer, veneration and contemplation.

If you wish to bring the blessings of the Goddess into your life, dedicate your altar to her by enshrining her image. This might be a reproduction of a fertility figure, or a

▷ Angels are believed to provide protection and guidance. An angelic altar brings loving support during times of sadness and loss.

ANIMAL SYMBOLISM

Images of animals can be used on the altar to symbolize an aspect of your character or to help you focus on a quality you desire.

BEAR: receptive female energy, earth wisdom, introspection.
BISON: wisdom of the elders.
CAT: independence, intuition.
DEER: security and protection.
DOG or WOLF: loyalty, family.
DOLPHIN: understanding.
EAGLE: divine and earthly power.
FROG: cleansing, emotional healing.
HARE: quickness of thought.
HERON: self-reliance.
HORSE: freedom, power.
LION: strength.
LIZARD: illusions, letting go.
OWL: magic, wisdom.
RABBIT: fertility.
ROBIN: new beginnings.
TURTLE: endurance, experience, knowledge.

statue or painting of one of the many aspects of the Goddess worshipped by ancient cultures, such as Isis the compassionate mother of the Egyptians, Athene the Greek goddess of wisdom and craft, or Diana, the moon deity who lights up the darkness within. By invoking the Goddess and seeking her ancient wisdom you will find an aspect of her in yourself. Bringing her into the heart of the home in this way upholds a tradition that has been practised throughout history.

Counsellors and guardians

If you call on a guardian angel for spiritual support, you can place a picture or figurine of a beautiful angel on your altar to focus your prayer. Photographs of loved ones who have died will remind you that they are still part of your life; pictures that show them full of happiness and vitality help you to remember your whole relationship with them, not just the fact that you have lost them. Seek their wisdom and advice as you remember them.

In the shamanic tradition, everyone has a spirit ally in the form of an animal. Your guardian animal could be one that you particularly identify with, or you may want to call upon an animal spirit whose energy can help you in a time of need. Placing an image on your altar will deepen your connection with your animal ally. Your prayers might be inspired by a picture of a soaring bird: birds are traditionally seen as spiritual messengers, flying between earth and heaven.

Gemstones and crystals

Crystals — points of sparkling light created in the darkness of the earth — are potent emblems of spiritual illumination, purity and durability. The ancient Greeks considered all quartz crystals to be fragments that had fallen from the perfect crystal of truth that resided on Mount Olympus. As well as being objects of great beauty, crystals and

△ The points of a crystal help to direct energy. They can also help to channel healing thoughts.

gemstones are storehouses of powerful energies, and magical powers of healing and protection have been ascribed to them. Each crystal is believed to have a distinct spiritual nature and to exert a specific influence on the human spirit; each has its own associations and symbolism. Place crystals to which you feel drawn on your altar to endow it with their special power.

△ A crystal's structure can serve to align and harmonize the physical and mental worlds.

Objects of symbolic value

Everyone has a collection of treasures that represent memories of close relationships and happy times, and such things have a place on a home altar. They probably already have their own special places, either on display like little shrines where we see them each day, or nestling secretly and safely where we can always find them when we feel the need to touch them and remember. A private arrangement of this kind can be a good place to start exploring a relationship with a personal altar.

A lock of hair, a baby's first shoes, or a trinket from a wedding cake are traditional mementos that many people keep all their lives. Other items are precious because they were gifts: they carry the memory of the giver, as well as the positive energy associated with the act of giving. Placing objects of symbolic value on an altar sets them in a new context that makes us see them afresh. It acknowledges the importance of all that they represent.

Seasonal symbols

Altars can change with the seasons, celebrating the coming of spring with fresh flowers and seeds, or ushering in the Christmas festivities with garlands of evergreens. Special seasonal items could be arranged on an altar in honour of the traditional festivals of the Celtic eightfold year. For city dwellers, especially, seasonal altars reaffirm a connection with nature.

△ Tiny items of personal significance can be kept safe on your altar in a pretty bag.

Abstract symbols

Symbols predate writing as a means of conveying ideas. Ancient symbols were carved, painted, stitched and worked in metal for magical purposes, to ward off evil or to invoke gods. Some signs, identified as archetypes, appear to be universally understood. A symbol gains its significance from the emotional and spiritual weight it carries. Like music and art, symbolism is a language of the emotions.

Some of the most compelling symbols are the simplest, such as the circle that represents the cycle of life, death and rebirth. The spiral, too, stands for the cycle of existence, but its outward motion also symbolizes growth and the energy of the vortex. In Celtic symbolism, the triple spiral stands for the three stages of life personified by the Triple Goddess: maiden, mother and crone.

The cross is the emblem of Christianity, and also represents the four cardinal directions. In pre-Columbian America the cross was a fertility symbol related to the four rain-bearing winds. The *ankh*, a cross surmounted by a loop, was an ancient Egyptian symbol of immortality.

The pentacle, or five-pointed star, is an ancient symbol of harmony and mystic power. When used magically it is inscribed on a disc. It is a female symbol related to the earth element.

Ancient graphic symbols such as these can bring their energy and associations to your altar. By painting or carving them yourself, you will enhance your connection with them: it is worth learning new craft skills to achieve this.

▽ Altars can provide a focus for poignant memories and remind us of the good in our lives.

RUNES AND THEIR MEANINGS

ᚠ FEOH: spiritual richness.

ᚢ UR: strength in a time of change.

ᚦ THORN: contemplation before action.

ᚪ ANSUR: messages and new opportunities.

ᚱ RAD: the wheel of life, a journey or quest.

ᚲ KEN: enlightenment and inspiration.

ᚷ GEOFU: a spiritual gift, love and partnership.

ᚹ WYNN: success and achievement.

ᚺ HAGALL: strength to face a challenge.

ᚾ NIED: need.

ᛁ IS: standstill, preparation before moving on.

ᛇ JARA: harvest, reward for past effort.

ᛃ EOH: transformation.

ᛈ PEORTH: choice, taking charge.

ᛉ ELHAZ: protection within.

ᛋ SIGEL: good fortune.

ᛏ TYR: dedication, perseverance.

ᛒ BEORC: new beginnings.

ᛖ EHWAZ: progress.

ᛗ MANN: destiny.

ᛚ LAGU: attunement to creation.

ᛜ ING: the inner spark.

ᛞ DAEG: the light.

ᛟ OTHEL: focus and freedom.

Runes

The runes are a sacred writing system of northern Europe, which, according to legend, appeared to the god Odin during a shamanic initiation rite. They were his gift of knowledge to humanity, and they are empowered with ancient wisdom. Runes can be used as guides for meditation and divination, as protective talismans and in wishing ceremonies.

Portable altars

Some people like to know that their personal altar is completely private to them. If you feel this way, you could arrange a beautiful small shrine inside a cupboard or box. A small wooden box makes a lovely altar, because you can lay out all your sacred things on the flat lid. It is also portable, so you can take it with you when travelling – especially useful if you are making a difficult trip and need spiritual support. Alternatively, when you leave home you could carry with you a crystal that you have programmed at your home altar (see *Rites and Ritual* at the end of this chapter).

△ A portable altar kit can be an excellent idea if you are often on the move, and wish to carry the essence of your home with you.

△ Runes are used for spiritual guidance, and can also add a symbolic message to an altar.

Candles and incense

Candles embody the positive symbolism of light as spiritual illumination, and the fragile candle flame is a powerful emblem of the individual soul, especially in a time of darkness and distress. Other lights, such as oil lamps and lanterns, can have a similar reassuring significance, and a perpetual flame on an altar stands for the constant presence of the divine.

Watching a lighted candle can be an aid to meditation and, like the candle flame, the fragrance of incense helps to focus the senses and calm chattering thoughts. Incense smoke has a symbolic status on the altar as an offering and is also used in ritual purification. It is an integral element of worship in many traditions.

Altar candles

The lighting of candles is a simple ceremonial act that initiates and hallows ritual. It acts as an announcement of the intention to worship. In the Catholic church, a prescribed number of candles must be lit before

each mass, the number varying depending on the solemnity of the service. It is common practice to light a candle and leave it to burn out before the shrine of a saint as an act of devotion, symbolizing both prayer and sacrifice. Candles are also used to mark rites of passage, from baptism to funerals. Placed around a coffin, their light is believed to protect the dead from evil during the vulnerable time of transition.

The Christian use of altar candles was adopted from older traditions, and candles have been significant in religion and magic since the earliest times. The ancient Egyptians, who practised dream incubation, would sit in a cave staring at a candle flame until they saw a deity in it. When they went to sleep the deity would answer their question.

The feast of Candlemas at the beginning of February was grafted on to the pagan fire festival Imbolc. A traditional feature was the blessing of all the candles that were to be used in the church for the rest of the year.

△ **Candle-gazing can increase concentration, and can be helpful when focus is required.**

Candlemas is a time of purification and dedication, and is a good time to clean and re-dedicate an altar.

△ **White candles represent purity and simplicity and can be used for any ceremony or ritual.**

△ **Resins produce impressive clouds of fragrant smoke, infusing the environment with scent.**

COLOUR ASSOCIATIONS FOR CANDLES

WHITE: spiritual enlightenment, healing, peace and purity; can be substituted for any other colour for ritual use.

YELLOW: intelligence, communication, concentration, movement.

ORANGE: attraction, stimulation, strength, luck.

GOLD: understanding, confidence, prosperity, cosmic influences; honours solar deities.

PINK: harmony, nurturing, family, affection.

RED: energy, life, courage, passion.

VIOLET or PURPLE: spirituality, inner harmony, wisdom.

INDIGO: cleansing, meditation.

BLUE: wisdom, inspiration, truth, healing; honours lunar deities.

GREEN: love, nature, renewal, abundance.

BROWN: home, wealth, stability, older family members.

SILVER or GREY: secrets, compromise.

BLACK: conclusions; banishes guilt, regret and negativity.

Magic and ritual

Traditional candle magic often involves writing the name of something you wish for on a piece of paper and then burning the paper in the candle flame, so that the wish is carried away in the smoke. In another candle charm, a symbol of the wish is engraved in the wax. As the candle burns down, the melted wax dripping down its

side may form an image to indicate how your wish might come true.

For ritual use, candles can be empowered by 'dressing' or anointing them with oil, to cleanse them of energies and influences from the past. The oil is wiped from the middle of the candle to the ends if the ritual aims to send energy out, or from the ends to the middle if the intention is to achieve or attract something.

In pagan tradition, the candle flame represents the element of fire, associated with life, creative energy and passion. Blowing candles out is said to be an affront to fire, and will have the effect of blowing away your intent or desire. It is best to let the candle burn down completely, although this is not always possible. Tibetan Buddhists consider that in blowing out a candle they are blowing away the breath of life, so pinch out the flame instead. For the same reason, incense sticks should be waved rather than blown before the altar.

Incense

The burning of incense on the altar is a gentle form of offering, with its associations of purity and sweetness. It clears the sacred space of invasive thoughts and images, giving a feeling of peace and serenity. It allows your spirit to soar above the mundane.

Combustible incense, in the form of joss-sticks and cones, is readily available.

◁ Incense comes in many forms, from cones to loose herbs and resins. All the different scents have particular associations and symbolism.

Alternatively, mixtures of fragrant resins, herbs and spices can be bought or prepared at home for burning on a charcoal block. For this you will need an incense burner, preferably with a stand or feet to protect the altar. Line the burner with a layer of sand to stabilize it and insulate it further. Concentrate on your intent as you light the incense, so that it is charged with your positive thoughts and the scented smoke drifts upwards carrying your prayers with it.

There may be times when you prefer to scent your altar with more delicate fragrances than incense. You can use essential oils in an aromatherapy burner, natural pot pourri mixtures or scented flowers.

INCENSE ASSOCIATIONS

COPAL: for honouring the gods, cleansing, and to bless love.

FRANGIPANI: for the blessing of friendship and love.

FRANKINCENSE: for cleansing and blessing, banishing bad influences and enhancing insight.

HONEYSUCKLE: for healing and psychic power.

JASMINE: for increasing sensitivity and to bless meditation.

LOTUS: for clearing the mind.

MUSK: for courage and vitality.

MYRRH: for purifying and cleansing of negative thoughts.

PATCHOULI: for grounding, fertility, protection and prosperity.

PINE: for strength and reversal of negative energies.

ROSE: for emotional healing and the expression of feelings.

SANDALWOOD: for protection, healing, and granting of wishes.

VANILLA: for rejuvenation, love and mental concentration.

WHITE SAGE: for purifying and cleansing sacred space.

The four elements

Natural processes are the basis of all existence, and a traditional way of understanding the workings of nature is through the physical elements: fire, air, water and earth. Ancient systems of thought looked for a way of describing the balance of nature that sustained the harmony of the world. The ancients knew the destructive potential of natural forces and concluded that a constant struggle for control was necessary to preserve the equilibrium of the universe: the imposition of order on the primeval state of chaos had to be the work of supernatural beings, and human co-operation with the gods was vital to maintain that order. The balance between the elements was seen as the basis of the cosmos.

According to this view, everything – each person, animal, plant, stone, thought – is a combination of the elements, blended in unique proportions. All four are essential to life, but to them must be added the all-important fifth element – the quintessence – which the Greek philosophers called ether. This is the spirit or cosmic energy that is the connecting power of the universe. Each of the physical elements is empowered by the pervasive influence of spirit.

△ Fire is hot and vibrant, honoured with bowls of hot spices such as cayenne or pepper.

▽ Air is changeable and quick: honour it with feathers and the smoke of incense.

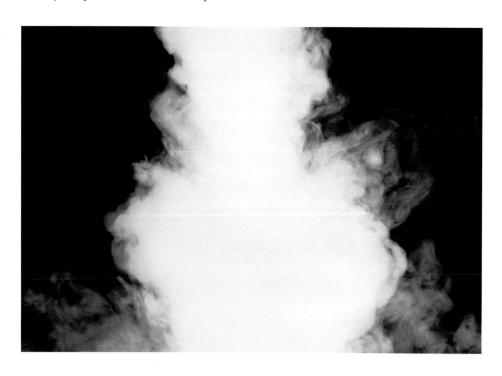

Correspondences

We see the universe with ourselves at its centre, and as we are bilaterally symmetrical we recognize four cardinal directions: in front, behind, left and right. These four directions are mirrored by the two poles of the earth's axis and the directions of the rising and setting sun.

The concept of the cardinal directions reflects an age-old understanding of the symmetry of the universe that has developed in many cultures. It is reflected, for instance, in the traditional medicine wheel of the native American shaman. Another example appears in a Chinese creation myth, according to which the world began when the cosmic giant Pangu died. His head became the mountain of the east, his feet the mountain of the west, and his two arms the mountains of the north and south. These sacred peaks marked the four cardinal directions and bounded the universe.

Each of the elements is associated with one of the directions: air rules the east, fire

▷ Water is cool and fluid, and is appropriately honoured with cool fragrances such as white sandalwood and jasmine.

THE ELEMENTS IN ALCHEMY

The four elements played a part in the secret process of alchemy, which was an attempt to create the magical elixir known as the Philosopher's Stone. With this, alchemists believed, would come the key to knowledge and enlightenment.

The elements were all contained in the 'first matter', or source material for the process. In myth, alchemy was said to have been the creation of the Egyptian god Thoth, and the original first matter was the fertile black silt of the Nile. Vital to the transformative process of alchemy were the three alchemical elements: salt (related to earth), mercury (related to both air and water) and sulphur (related to fire). The alchemists believed that if they could purify all these ingredients sufficiently and synthesize them correctly, they would be able to produce the Philosopher's Stone.

▽ Earth is solid and cold: it can be honoured with offerings of crystals and salt – the sacred symbol of this element.

the south, water the west and earth the north. Chinese philosophy follows a slightly different scheme and includes metal and wood (as elements). Fire is again the element of the south. Wood goverens the east, metal the west and water the north. Earth lies at the centre and represents stability.

When the early astrologers mapped the heavens and plotted the zodiac, the relationship between directions and elements meant that each of the signs was governed by an element and exhibited its character-istics. As well as ruling a direction, each element is identified with a season and a stage of human life. Each one governs the area of life in which it is dominant: for instance, air is the element of ideas while earth presides over the material world. The traditional symbolism of the elements also includes connections with magical tools, musical sounds, colours, deities, animals, plants, and stones. Any of these symbols can be used ritually on an altar to harness the elemental energy you wish to invoke.

ZODIAC SIGNS AND THE ELEMENTS

FIRE (Aries, Leo, Sagittarius): energetic, innovative and volatile, lacking in perseverance.
EARTH (Taurus, Virgo, Capricorn): practical, cautious and reliable, lacking in imagination.
AIR (Gemini, Libra, Aquarius): intellectual, rational, lacking in intuition.
WATER (Cancer, Scorpio, Pisces): emotional, sympathetic, receptive, illogical.

Rites and ritual

Setting up an altar at home is one step on your spiritual path, but the journey continues. Although your journey is an inward one, a sacred place serves as a reminder of the way. Each time you use it in personal ceremonies and rituals you strengthen the positive energy it holds for you.

If you share the altar with your partner or family, the occasions on which you come together for worship and ritual help to reinforce the bonds between you. Or you may think of your altar as a private and personal space, somewhere you can go when you are angry or upset to be quiet and restore your calm and inner strength. Use it to nourish your soul and help you unwind at the end of a tiring day. At difficult times of transition, use it as a support, and at times of peace, go to the altar to give thanks.

Preparation

To prepare for your ceremonies, you should purify your sacred space by cleaning the room and clearing away clutter, and cleanse yourself so that you feel refreshed and energized. See that the altar is clean and free of dust, that the flowers are fresh and candles

▽ **Calming the mind with meditation helps to cope with stress, and builds inner strength.**

△ **Sage gets its name from *saga*, meaning 'wise woman', and burning it summons protection.**

new. Burn some incense or white sage to clear away any negative energy from the area.

If you include crystals on your altar, cleanse them to clear past vibrations so that they become personal to you. You can do this in various ways: smoke is a gentle cleanser, or they can be placed in sunlight or moonlight, or washed in rain or spring water.

It is a good idea to devise a formal beginning for your time before the altar: light a candle or some incense to quieten your thoughts and prepare you to concentrate all your energy on the subject of your meditation or prayer. Focusing on deep, relaxed breathing helps to still your mind.

▽ **Singing bowls can produce a variety of sound vibrations that touch the body with resonance.**

◁ An offering of salt made to an earth goddess such as Gaia helps to build a close relationship with the earth.

▽ Mark the beginning or end of a ritual by ringing a bell or some chimes.

Daily ritual

Greeting the morning with a small ritual is a positive way to start a new day, and doing this before an altar sanctifies the act. If you practise yoga, for instance, you can perform your salutations to the sun in your sacred space. The ritual will strengthen your spiritual bond with creation while the movements invigorate your body.

Remember that you can change the format of your worship freely, as your needs and ideas change: you are not just an observer, as in a formal religious ritual. You might wish to read a text that inspires you, or recite a poem that helps you express your emotions. Singing, striking a singing bowl, playing a musical instrument or listening to music could form part of your ritual.

Prayer and meditation

If you are accustomed to saying daily prayers, or spending a particular period of time in meditation, your altar can become the focus of these regular practices. Prayer and meditation are complementary routes to spiritual development. As a request for help or guidance, or thanksgiving, prayer is active, while meditation is a passive exercise in contemplation, quietening the mind to increase its receptivity and allow the subconscious to surface.

Using an affirmation can help to focus your meditation. Create a thought that feels right to you: it needn't describe your present reality, but the reality you dream of. The affirmation is a way to make your dream real. Repeat the positive thought again and again, silently or aloud, to allow it to sink into your unconscious mind.

Programming a crystal

You can use the energy of your affirmation to programme a crystal on your altar (choose one that has properties appropriate to your particular goal, such as rose quartz for love or citrine for abundance). Hold the crystal in both hands and gaze into it as you concentrate on your wish. Breathe deeply and each time you inhale repeat the affirmation and picture what you want. As you exhale, project your desire into the crystal. You can also write your wish on a piece of paper and leave it under the crystal.

If you are travelling, or when you go to work each day, keep the programmed crystal near you by carrying it in a small bag.

Offerings

As part of your ceremony, place an offering on your altar as an expression of gratitude for the blessings of your life. Leaving a gift for another person on the altar for a while before you give it will endow it with positive energy and reinforce its value as a token of love. Adopt a way of closing your ceremony that you can repeat each time. Play a piece of music, say a farewell prayer, a thank you, or simply "amen", to give you a feeling of completion.

△ A prayer can be as simple as a few moments of silent communion with the spirit.

Altars of the Air

The lightness and clarity of the air element governs the realms of the mind, imagination and communication. Its ethereal nature inspires the creation of altars dedicated to mental power and intellectual challenges.

The element of air

△ The air element corresponds with the east, the direction of the rising sun, and with the morning.

Air is the element of life and breath – when we cease to breathe, life ends. Speediest and most ethereal of the elements, it rules the east, the direction of the sunrise. Because it is associated with the new day and with the freshness of the new year, air symbolizes new beginnings, enterprise, infancy and the generative energy of the seed. It is creative, focused, aware.

In the form of wind, air may be a gentle, cooling breeze or it may have the destructive force of a hurricane. Its energy is projective. Because air is the element of the four winds, it governs movement and is associated with travel, freedom and new discoveries. It is also the element of thought and ideas – the fresh, moving force of the open mind, of intellect and the imagination.

▽ The fresh, fast-moving element of air helps us to disperse the clouds of ignorance and doubt.

▽ Creatures of the air, birds symbolize the connection between earth and heaven.

▷ **Use incense and yellow flowers and candles on your altar to symbolize the qualities of air.**

Those in whom air is the dominant element are rational and analytical.

In daily life the areas governed by air include workplaces, offices, meeting rooms, schools and libraries, as well as places concerned with travel, such as railway stations and airports. It presides over the eastern quarter of a room or building. In the natural world, air's places are mountain tops, windy plains and clear or cloudy skies.

The power of the mind can include psychic ability, and air governs the arts of divination and visualization. It enhances positive thinking, allowing the mind to expand into wider realms, and to connect personal experience with the universal.

Gods of the air

Deities associated with air are Shu, Thoth, Hermes and Mercury. Shu was the Egyptian god of the air who, with his consort Tefnut (the goddess of moisture), created the earth and sky. The Egyptian moon god Thoth was the sacred scribe of Osiris. As the god of wisdom, he was

endowed with secret knowledge. It was said that his book of magic contained spells that would give the user power over all the gods, and that between them his books contained all the wisdom of the world. He eventually became associated with the Greek god Hermes, the messenger of the Olympian gods, who could travel as fast as thought.

Hermes was versatile and changeable, eloquent and inventive, the personification of consciousness. His quick wits and slippery character made him the patron of thieves and merchants as well as travellers. His Roman equivalent was Mercury, whose cult spread widely among the Celtic and Germanic peoples of the Roman Empire. The latter identified him with Wotan or Odin, the god of speech, breath, wind, storm and magic. Mercury gave us the word 'mercurial' to describe a volatile, lively, quicksilver character. Invoke these deities to bless an altar with the energy of air.

THE ATHAME

Wiccans use this ritual knife to draw circles, control elemental spirits and direct energy during ceremonies. It has a dark handle and a double edge. It is seldom used for actual cutting, and would never be used as a weapon. It represents the masculine force on the altar.

AIR CORRESPONDENCES

DIRECTION: east.
SEASON: spring.
TIME: dawn.
MOON PHASE: new.
PLANETS: sun, Mercury, Uranus.
GENDER: masculine.
COLOURS: yellow and violet.
SENSES: hearing and smell.
MAGICAL TOOLS: wand, athame, sword.
INSTRUMENTS: wind instruments.
CREATURES: birds, winged insects.
NATURAL SYMBOLS: feathers, incense smoke, fragrant flowers.
TREES: elder, eucalyptus.
HERBS: comfrey, lavender, mint.
INCENSE: sandalwood, lemon.
MINERALS: mercury, aventurine, topaz.
SIGNS: Gemini, Libra, Aquarius.
ARCHANGEL: Raphael.

An altar for new beginnings

The most challenging times in life are those of transition. At moments when we are breaking with old customs and habits, or taking on new responsibilities, we need a boost to our self-confidence to stop us feeling uncertain, isolated or afraid. The established routines of our everyday lives have to be abandoned, and we may doubt our ability to meet a new challenge. We need to feel supported.

In traditional societies, the moment of setting out on a new chapter in life is invariably marked by some form of ritual that offers this kind of spiritual support, but in modern times many of the old ceremonies have been curtailed or lost. Others that do survive – such as weddings – have become so commercialized that their spiritual value can be hard to hold on to.

A simple ceremony at your altar will help you focus your thoughts and find the resolution to make a bold leap into the new. If you have just fallen in love you could be entering a new relationship that will be central to your whole future. If you are expecting a child the focus of your life is about to change radically. If you are moving house or starting a new job, you will be embarking on a series of new encounters and opportunities to shape your future.

△ **The yellow triangle and violet circle both symbolize the air element.**

◁ **For new beginnings, such as the dawn of spring, yellow and violet flowers are ideal as they are the colours associated with a fresh start.**

Sometimes the impetus towards a fresh start has to arise from sadder circumstances, such as divorce, children growing up and leaving home, or moving to a new area, away from people you love. At such times, the transition is one from grief and loss to healing and moving forward. The creative act of setting up an altar can be part of the process of transformation.

Invoke the element of air to inspire you with confidence and hope for a new beginning. Set your altar in the easterly quarter of a room, so that when you stand before it you are facing east, the direction of the sunrise. If possible, arrange it under a window so that it is bathed in the morning sunshine. Place a bell on the altar.

To symbolize new growth and natural energy you could add a vase of flowers: choose violet and yellow flowers, the colours of the air element, to help you focus your intent. Burn incense containing rosemary to clarify your thoughts. White candles represent new beginnings and clear vision.

◁ The number three is associated with manifestations – ringing your bell three times will help to call new realities into your life.

AN INCENSE MIXTURE FOR FOCUS

Incense is a tool of the air element, and will help to clarify your thoughts.

2 parts dried rosemary
1 part dried thyme
1 part lemongrass
Few drops rosemary essential oil

Pound all the dry ingredients together using a pestle and mortar, then add the essential oil. Mix the oil in well with your fingertips. Burn a few pinches of incense on the altar, using a charcoal block.

Ritual for a new start

The time of the waxing moon is the period between the new and the full moon, when the half moon can be seen in the sky during the first part of the night. This is the time of new beginnings, and during this period you can perform a simple ritual to help you approach the next part of your life with confidence. As you meditate before your altar, focus on your hopes and wishes for the future. Write these down on a piece of yellow paper cut into a triangle, and lay the triangle on a larger violet or blue circlet of paper or cloth on the altar.

Place the bell on top of the piece of paper. Each morning of the period of the waxing moon – as near sunrise as possible – come to the altar and ring the bell three times as you visualize your hopes and wishes being realized and achieved.

▽ Burn a pinch or two of incense in the morning to cleanse your mind for the day ahead.

THE SEASON OF NEW BEGINNINGS

The pagan festival of Ostara is celebrated at the Vernal Equinox, around 21 March in the northern hemisphere and 23 September in the southern hemisphere, when day and night are of equal length and the sun begins its ascendancy: a time of balance and regeneration. Ostara signals the return of spring and is a festival of new life and fertility. This is the time to plant seeds and initiate new plans. An altar to celebrate Ostara could be decorated with spring flowers and herbs: celandine, daffodil, primroses, violets, sage, tansy and thyme. Yellow and green candles represent clear focus, optimism and new growth.

An altar for meditation

Creating a personal altar in a garden is a rewarding way to acknowledge our connection with nature, and provides a tranquil space for quiet thought and meditation. It can be a breathing space, both literally and metaphorically, where the freshness of the breeze, the scent of leaves and flowers and the sound of birds inspire us with a sense of gratitude and awareness.

Meditation is a way of focusing the mind, stilling the endless mental chatter that distracts us from concentrated thought. It is not a way of escaping from the reality of our everyday responsibilities. It increases awareness and enables us to live fully in each moment with contentment and serenity.

According to Zen Buddhism, the practice of gardening is itself an active form of meditation. The size of the garden is not important: the message of Zen is that the large can be experienced in the small, and

▽ Taking a little time with your designs helps the mind become relaxed and centred.

△ The patterns you create in your miniature garden will contain potent messages to your subconscious, and will help to integrate your inner and outer worlds.

the meaning of the whole world can be seen in a grain of sand. The garden is the universe in microcosm. The concept can be adapted to your own garden, where you can fashion a serene space for meditation with stones, gravel and moss, inspired by the temple gardens of Japan.

Gardens of contemplation

Respect for nature and a sense of connectedness with natural cycles are basic tenets of Zen Buddhist thought. Zen arrived in Japan from China in the 11th century, and its emphasis on contemplation and tranquillity found a natural counterpart in the Japanese love of simplicity. Buddhist monks applied the concepts of Zen to their daily

▷ **Once you are satisfied with the patterns you have made, move on to your meditation.**

lives, and designed their living quarters and gardens in accordance with them, producing simple, peaceful spaces for meditation in perfect accord with nature.

Zen gardens are often conceived as miniature re-creations of natural scenes, such as mountains and forests. Composed of simple elements such as moss, leaves, stones and water, they are timeless havens of silent contemplation. Paths meander, and a stream may be crossed by a zig-zagging 'eightfold' bridge, forcing the visitor to move slowly and appreciate each vista.

In a 'dry' garden, a natural scene is re-created without water. The rocks are arranged with artful judgement to appear as if naturally strewn in beds of pale gravel, which is carefully raked. The elements of such a garden are symbolic: the stones represent the great age of the universe and the swirling patterns in the gravel imitate the river flowing around them. Some stones lie hidden or partly buried in the gravel, so that the eye is led down beneath the surface, just as in meditation Buddhists look within themselves to seek enlightenment.

Symbols also abound in the plants that grow in Japanese gardens, and these ideas can be used to enhance the significance of elements in your own outdoor sacred space. Evergreen pines, for example, stand for longevity, and the fleeting, delicate plum blossom that appears in the cold of early spring is a symbol of courage.

FORM AND EMPTINESS

The serenity of a Zen garden has an almost hypnotic effect, and you can use its combination of form and emptiness as a starting point for a meditation. When you have worked on your Zen garden, and created a pattern that springs from your inner consciousness, sit back and contemplate it. Empty your mind of its clutter and confusion and absorb the simplicity and peace of the natural forms in front of you.

A miniature Zen garden

You can create a garden on a miniature scale, following the ideas of Zen, on a wooden platter or tray. The process of creating and working in the garden itself becomes a form of meditation, helping to soothe the mind and reduce stress.

Fill the tray with sand or fine gravel, and arrange some groups of beautiful pebbles in it. The stones you use could be found anywhere: in the street, in the park, on the beach. Once you begin to look at them properly you will be amazed at their beauty and form. Gazing on the stones you choose for your garden – all of them millions of years old – may prompt you to see your life in a new perspective.

You may decide to make your garden entirely with sand and pebbles. This art of gardening is called *bonseki* in Japan, and is the 'dry' equivalent of bonsai. Or you can add fresh flowers or small plants to represent living natural forms. Use a stick or a small rake to create spirals and circles in the sand around the stones and plants. These patterns can be smoothed away and redrawn whenever you come to the garden: they evoke the fluidity of the present moment and the impermanence of human life.

Try to dedicate a few moments a day to contemplation. Even if your time for meditation is short, the garden can become a small oasis of peace and quiet where you can find some spiritual freedom.

An altar for motivation

We are all motivated by many different things: physical and emotional drives, the need to survive, self-satisfaction and pleasure, our values, interests and ambitions, rewards, fears and established habits. Often the different influences that press upon us oppose each other in confusing and defeating ways. It's very easy to spend too much time and energy on activities that seem urgent but aren't really important. Instead we need to concentrate on the issues that may not seem so urgent, but are actually much more important to us, such as clarifying what we want our lives to be, fostering good relationships with others, and preserving our health by exercising, eating properly and getting enough rest.

Motivation comes with feeling capable, self-directed and hopeful, and challenging and positive goals are motivating in themselves. Pinning your hopes on impossible dreams, on the other hand, simply becomes frustrating: deep down you know you will not succeed, so you build in the idea of failure before you begin.

It's important to set goals that are achievable but that stretch your capabilities: this is a fine balance and needs careful thought –

◁ Choose incense ingredients that mirror and magnify your intent or goal.

△ Orange or yellow flowers on your motivation altar will inspire creative thinking.

about what you really want to do, and about yourself. You have to listen to your inner voice, and face honestly how you are feeling about a situation: sometimes an apparent lack of motivation conceals anxiety about beginning a difficult task. Once you acknowledge that you are fearful it is easier to face up to your fear and see the problem objectively. Break a seemingly impossible task down into tiny steps and do the first one – once you've started, the next step ceases to feel so momentous.

Lack of motivation can often stem from simple fatigue. If you're feeling frantic, don't be afraid to take a break. Stand back from your situation and re-organize it. However busy you are, make time for exercise, proper meals and sleep. Don't wear yourself out meeting other people's expectations if they are unreasonable.

Moving forward

Making an altar invites change into your life. It is a positive statement that you intend to focus your inner resources and move forward. With most of the things that we find difficult, the hardest part of all is beginning: the creation of an altar is an act of faith that gets you started and underlines the seriousness of your endeavours. The altar is a

INCENSE FOR MOTIVATION

2 parts cinnamon
2 parts frankincense grains
1 part nutmeg
1 part allspice
1 part ginseng
1 part juniper berries
Few drops frankincense essential oil

Pound all the dry ingredients with a pestle and mortar, then add the essential oil. Burn a few grains at a time on a charcoal block.

tangible expression of your intent to set aside time to evaluate your dreams and wishes. As a place where you can contemplate your life, it will help you to set worthwhile goals and to achieve them.

As air is the element of the intellect and the imagination, of dreams and ideas, its influence is important in an altar dedicated to motivation. When you feel sluggish and unable to get going, visualize a fresh breeze blowing away the cobwebs of your mind, bringing clear thought and inspiration. Add a little fire to your altar, too, to inspire you with drive and creativity. Fire is the element of change and helps to break old habits.

Your altar for motivation should sparkle with energy and light. Place it in a sunny window so that when you come to it in the morning the freshness and beauty of the new day greet you and fill you with optimism. If possible, use the windowsill as the altar, and on fine days open the window to let in the morning air.

Choose a beautiful, shimmering piece of fabric, such as a length of organza shot with gold, to use as an altar cloth, and decorate the altar with yellow and orange flowers. Yellow candles will help you to concentrate single-mindedly on your goals. Include an incense burner on which you can sprinkle a few grains each morning. Your altar ritual can include reviewing the achievements of the previous day and writing out your list of goals for the forthcoming day.

A TIMETABLE FOR ACHIEVEMENT

Planning your day effectively helps you to stay in control, which increases motivation. It also helps you to decide on priorities. Get into the habit of making weekly and daily schedules that are based on realistic goals, rather than a wish list that is impossible to achieve. Set clear starting and stopping times for work sessions, with proper breaks. Include plenty of time for rest and recreation, and allow some flexibility for unforeseen demands.

Altars of Fire

The spark of imagination sets light to our powers of creativity and ignites the passions. Use the heat and intensity of fire to create vivid altars that will motivate you to achieve your ambitions.

The element of fire

△ The turbulent, uncontrollable energy of lava illustrates fire's governance over the passions.

Fire is both creative and destructive. It can cleanse and purify, but it consumes: it is the only one of the four elements that cannot exist without feeding on something else. It creates warm, welcoming homes and cooks our food, but it is dangerous and can get out of control. It has the power to transform everything it touches.

Fire rules the south, the direction of the sun's fiercest heat (in the northern hemi-sphere), and it is related to motivation, creativity and passion. Its energy is quick-acting, forceful and positive and its power can be frightening. It symbolizes the inner child, the spirit within and the creative spark. Because it is the element of the passions, it gives courage and strength to fight for faith and quality of life. Those in whom it is dominant are passionate and intense. Fire consumes obstacles to faith and trust, and banishes negativity.

Areas governed by fire are kitchens, fire-places and boiler rooms, gyms and athletics fields, and creative spaces such as studios and playrooms. Fire presides over the southern quarter of a room or building. In the nat-ural world, its places are deserts, hot springs and volcanoes.

Fire governs the sense of sight, it also inspires the need to offer and accept the power of touch. It is the element of physi-cal challenge, sensation and sexual energy. It celebrates life.

▽ Fire can be dangerous and destructive, but it may burn away obstacles to new growth.

FIRE METAL

One of the fire metals, iron, is found on earth in its pure form only in meteorites. It is present in our blood, and is essential for physical energy and clear thinking. Wearing it as a talisman is said to increase physical strength. In some cultures, an iron talisman is worn as protec-tion against evil or negative energy: for this reason Sikhs wear an iron or steel bangle called a *kara* on their right wrist at all times.

▷ The lighting of a candle on the altar is a simple act that initiates ceremony as well as honouring the element of fire.

Gods and goddesses of fire

Some of the deities associated with fire are Re, Sekhmet, Apollo and Lugh.

Re was worshipped by the ancient Egyptians as their pre-eminent solar deity. As a creator god, he brought order out of chaos – from his tears, the first human beings were formed. He was born each morning and journeyed across the sky in his solar boat, entering the underworld each night to do battle with the cosmic serpent, Apep. 'Son of Re' was one of the titles bestowed on the pharaoh. Re's daughter was the sun goddess Sekhmet, 'the Powerful One', who was usually portrayed with the head of a lioness. Re sent Sekhmet as his 'Eye', the terrible burning power of the sun, to punish the wickedness of humankind, but at the last moment saved his creation from total destruction by diverting Sekhmet's frenzied rage. Sekhmet was the terrifying aspect of Hathor, the goddess of joy and maternal love.

In Greek mythology, the sun was guided across the sky by Apollo, who also represents light, truth and clarity. He was the god of medicine and of music, and was the patron of the nine Muses, the embodiments of the creative imagination. The Celtic sky-god Lugh was a deity of the sun and the weather, and his spear is sometimes seen as a fork of lightning. As the god of skills and arts, he could be honoured by an offering of a creative work. The pagan summer festival of Lughnasadh, celebrated at the beginning of the harvest, is held in his name. Invoke these deities to bless an altar with the energy of fire.

▽ The lion is a universal symbol of strength and courage. Medieval alchemists also used it to represent transformation through fire.

FIRE CORRESPONDENCES
DIRECTION: south.
SEASON: summer.
TIME: midday.
MOON PHASE: first quarter.
PLANETS: Mars, Pluto.
GENDER: masculine.
COLOURS: red and orange.
SENSE: sight.
MAGICAL TOOLS: candles, lanterns, solar icons, wand.
INSTRUMENTS: stringed instruments.
CREATURES: dragon, snake, lion, ram, phoenix.
NATURAL SYMBOLS: flame, lava.
TREES: oak, hawthorn.
HERBS: basil, bay, garlic, hyssop, juniper, rosemary, rue.
INCENSE: frankincense, cinnamon, basil.
MINERALS: brass, gold, iron, fire opal, garnet, hematite, red jasper, sardonyx, flint.
SIGNS: Aries, Leo, Sagittarius.
ARCHANGEL: Michael.

An altar for creativity

Assembling a personal altar is a wonderful act of self-expression, and is in itself a creative act. Dedicating the altar to creativity recognizes and honours your powers of invention and originality. It is a very positive way to affirm your own talent. If you dream of a creative endeavour but have not dared to pursue it for fear that you will fail, bringing your dreams to your altar can help to dispel your inhibitions.

The spirit of creation flows through every one of us. We may describe it as divine inspiration, chi, life force or quintessence, but it is the energy that we put into everything we create – whether that thing is a sculpture, a letter or a meal. No narrow definitions apply here: creativity should not be confined to writing, painting or other 'artistic' pursuits. It is important for everything we do to be approached creatively, giving spiritual value to even the most mundane tasks.

Inspiration

To inspire literally means to 'breathe into', and the ancient Greek poets, whose word it is, would invoke one of the nine Muses to inspire them. They saw themselves as channels through which the divine voice could be heard. As a focus of positive energy,

△ The creative altar should be filled with colours of the rainbow, inviting variety, vibrancy and colour into your own world as a result.

▽ Focus your creative altar by adding elements that symbolize your own artistic endeavour in your chosen field.

the altar is a place to tune into the creative spirit and call on it to inspire us.

In addition to inspiration, the creative process demands hard work, discipline, judgement and the courage to make mistakes and learn from them. At the altar we can find the motivation to acquire the skills we need to express ourselves. In our own sacred space we can leave behind the limits of self-consciousness, so that our open minds attract fresh ideas like magnets, faster than they can be expressed. It is in this state of intuitive awareness – a form of meditation – that creativity flows.

Creating the altar

Make your altar a thing of shimmering beauty to awaken your senses and fill you with the joy of creation. Dress it with a rainbow of colour and let its flamboyance give you the confidence to express yourself in other ways as you have here. The objects you choose to put on it can reflect whichever creative opportunities you want to explore, such as brushes and paints for artistic endeavour, or pens and paper if you are searching for the courage to express yourself in writing. Use this special place to try out your dreams, and bring your own creations to beautify your altar.

An altar for fertility

The most profound act of creation is that of new life itself. If you are trying to have a baby, the energy of your creativity altar can be devoted to your desire to conceive. Some of the world's most ancient altars were erected for this purpose, celebrating the fertility of the earth and of women with the element of fire, the spark of life.

If this is the special purpose of your altar, include on it objects that speak of abundance and new growth, such as seeds and flowers, and add some beautiful images of parenthood and babies. You could also include a figure of the great Goddess to ally yourself with her fertile power.

IMBOLC: THE LIGHT OF INSPIRATION

The festival of the return of light, at the beginning of February, honours the Celtic triple goddess Brigid, a fire deity, and celebrates her union with the god of light. It is a time of inspiration and creativity, when rituals are performed to bless new love, fertility, and the planning of new projects. Imbolc is predominantly a female festival, and Brigid blesses women's self-expression and creativity.

At this season, the goddess is honoured in her maiden aspect as the patron of inspiration and poetry. By tradition, if a white cloth is left outside overnight at Imbolc, the goddess will bless it with inspiration.

THE FULL MOON

When the moon is full, its energy is opposed to that of the sun as they are on opposite sides of the earth, and the moon rises as the sun sets. The time of the full moon is therefore a period of high potency. It is the best time for rituals at the altar to encourage fertility, passion and abundance. In ancient times, women would rise before dawn on the day of the full moon and go into the fields. There they would wash themselves in the morning dew, asking the moon to bless them with children.

An altar for positive outcomes

It has long been acknowledged that if you have a clear idea of what you want you are far more likely to achieve it. Thought is a form of energy, and positive thinking contributes energetically to the fulfilment of your desire. Just as an artist has an idea that leads to the creation of a work of art, ideas are the first step to creating your future.

You should begin by thinking clearly about what you want. This is an effective way to make things happen, rather than simply allowing them to happen to you. Ideas, thoughts and wishes are running through our minds all day, but often we hardly give our-selves the chance to hold on to them before they disappear. Voicing such thoughts in a conscious way harnesses their energy to help us work towards their successful fulfilment.

When you are facing a challenging situation it is easy to focus on all the difficulties that might arise and to become preoccupied with the chance of failure. While it's important to have a realistic idea of what you are facing, the negative energy created by worry and fear can be paralysing. You may spend more time identifying all that could go wrong than in constructing a detailed and positive image of the outcome you want. A daily ceremony at your altar helps to focus your energy on what you want to happen.

The life-affirming qualities of an altar dedicated to the element of fire will support you and give you the courage to achieve success. Place on your altar images that symbolize courage and strength, such as a lion, a picture of a great oak tree or an object made of its wood. An image of the Archangel Michael would invoke his aid: he is the angel of fire and prince of the sun, who assists in matters of achievement and ambition.

▽ **Use orange candles and images of strength and power on an altar to ensure success.**

▽ **Invoke the aid of the Archangel Michael on your fire altar by lighting a candle in front of his image. The image of a lion is also a potent one for a fire altar.**

HERBS AND SPICES FOR SUCCESS

BASIL: gives protection, repels negativity and brings wealth. Leaves carried in the pocket bring luck in gambling, scattered on a shop floor they bring business success.

BERGAMOT: attracts success and prosperity. Rubbing the oil on money before it is spent will ensure the return of riches; the leaves in a purse attract money.

CINNAMON: draws money, protection and success.

CLOVE: banishes any hostile or negative forces and helps to gain whatever is sought.

VERVAIN: attracts money, protection; transforms enemies into friends.

△ **When burning a wish it is vital to ensure that the paper is completely burnt to ashes.**

TURQUOISE: THE LUCKY STONE

A popular amulet, turquoise has many protective qualities. It is said to guard its owner against ill-health and poverty, and to guarantee success in any field. The Aztecs tied turquoises to their weapons to make them more effective in battle. It attracts new friends, brings joy and increases beauty. As a gift, it bestows wealth and happiness on the receiver.

A ceremony for success

Use an orange candle for your ritual, because orange is the colour of ambition, goals and success. It has the power to draw good things to it and to change luck. Anoint the candle with oil to charge it with your personal vibrations and make the ceremony more effective. Using a few drops of bergamot essential oil, wipe the candle from the base to the middle and then from the wick to the middle – concentrate on your desire as you do this so that it is transmitted to the candle, and hold the candle so that you make the strokes towards your body, as you are intending to draw success towards you.

Place the candle in the centre of the altar. Arrange basil leaves around its base like the rays of the sun, and use cloves to make a spiral pattern around the candle, symbolizing growth and energy. (Knocking anything over on the altar might make you feel less confident of success, so avoid this mischance by arranging everything carefully.)

As you stand before the altar and light the candle, focus all your thoughts on achieving the result you desire. You can also write down your wish on a piece of paper, fold it twice and leave it under the candle. Or burn the paper in the candle flame so that the wish is carried away on the smoke, all the time thinking clearly about what you want. Empowered by your magical efforts, you can follow them up with practical strategies to achieve the right outcome.

Altar for achieving goals

A period of stillness before a personal altar offers time to reflect on all the blessings of our lives, and to be grateful. It is also a time to find out about our true needs, which are yearning to be heard amidst the clamour of worldly ambition. When we give ourselves the space to listen to our inner selves, we may realize that we are pursuing goals that are not really fulfilling: perhaps work leaves too little time for relationships, family life or creativity; or perhaps it is no longer satisfying, and new qualifications would lead to a more challenging career.

Wherever our real ambitions lie, striving for achievement is necessary if our lives are to be fruitful and valuable. If we aim for nothing, we are always certain to hit it. And if we don't set our own priorities, someone else will. So setting out the things we want to achieve over the next week, month, year, or five years is a valuable exercise in estab-

△ **Frankincense attracts energy and power; surround the bowl with oak leaves for strength.**

▽ **As you write down your wishes, think carefully about the results you really want to achieve.**

SETTING GOALS

•Visualize your long-term goals and set short-term targets – weekly or monthly – to help you get there.

• Set specific daily goals to keep you motivated.

• Goals should stretch you, but not defeat you before you begin. If you make them too easy, they won't motivate you. Make each goal a challenging and positive one.

• Limit the number of your stated goals. Make sure they don't clash with each other, and that they don't interfere with other priorities in different areas of your life.

• Write a list down and leave it in an obvious place so you see it each day.

• Re-examine what you want from time to time. If your goals seem unrealistic, you can change them.

• Give yourself small rewards for each of your achievements.

lishing what is most important and finding realistic ways to make it happen. If we have only good intentions but do nothing to bring them about, the results will be remorse and regret. Achieving something that we want to do is a great boost to confidence and self-esteem, helping us to raise our sights to even higher goals. Aspirations need not be set in stone: they need re-evaluating as we learn from experiences, and as our outlook and priorities change.

A useful way to set yourself on the right course is to visualize the result you desire as if it has already happened. If your goal is to get a new job, you can visualize yourself opening the letter that has arrived to tell you it is yours. If your goal is a return to health and fitness, visualize yourself striding up a hill or running across a beach. If you are trying to pass your driving test, imagine yourself at the wheel of your own car. Hold on to your vision for as long as you can, so that it sinks from your conscious into your

▷ **Visualize your goals, but always be open to new influences and sensitive to others' needs.**

unconscious mind, forming a pattern into which you can grow. Each time you visit your altar, perform this visualization exercise to sanctify your intent and inform it with spirit. Even if there are times when you seem to be making no progress, your spirit will still be moving you forward in the direction you have chosen.

An altar for worldly success

For material achievements in your everyday life, such as money-making and success at work, include earth as well as fire on your altar. Earth is the element of stability and prosperity, and supports us in taking responsibility for our own destiny. Use the colours of the land, such as olive green and russet, and place on the altar two green candles and the materials of the earth, such as salt, stone and earth itself.

Place a bowl of the fire incense, frankincense, on the altar and use this for your rituals. Write your goals on a piece of paper and put the folded paper into the bowl of frankincense. As it sits there, visualize the realization of your ambitions. Try to imagine the successful outcome rather than the process of getting there. When you have fixed the images in your mind take the piece of paper and burn it in the flame of the candle. To finish, pinch out the candles and take a few moments to gather your thoughts.

A wishing box

Another way of working towards your goals is to create a wishing box. Write down your wishes and then keep them in a special wooden box on your altar. Surround the box with oak leaves, to sanctify and protect your dreams. The sacred oak will aid your rituals with its strength, and bring the promise of success.

Keep some frankincense in your wishing box. This most ancient incense has been burnt on the altars of many cultures to summon the aid of the divine. Its uplifting scent banishes negative thoughts and promotes success. Take a few grains from the box each day and burn them on charcoal as you visualize your goal.

▽ **Write a list of your goals, and when you have fixed them in your mind, burn the list in the candle flame on your altar.**

AN OFFICE ALTAR

Creating an altar in the office or workplace is a good way to help you achieve your working goals, and help keep you focused on the tasks at hand. It can be especially helpful if your office is in an environment charged with the energy of electronic equipment, and insulated from fresh air and sunlight. The harmonious influence of a sacred space helps to focus your thoughts on the essentials of life in the midst of stressful situations. Even a small arrangement on or near your desk – such as a picture of a beautiful landscape, a plant and a crystal – will introduce the sacred energy of the natural world.

An altar to the sun

The sun is a central symbol of creative energy, and has been an object of worship since the earliest times. The ancients recognized that without the sun, there would be no life. It is the giver of light, heat and fire: as light, it symbolizes knowledge and truth, and as heat and fire it stands for vitality and passion. In Celtic belief, fire was thought to have been brought to earth from the sun by a sacred bird – a swallow, swift or wren.

The sun provides the rhythmic structure of life on earth. It governs the annual cycle of the seasons and controls our biological rhythms as we wake and sleep each day. We are creatures of the light. Even in the modern world where we can switch on artificial light and heat whenever we need it, we still

▽ **Use herbs and spices that reflect and evoke heat on your solar altar.**

△ **Gold is the colour and metal of the male in its purest form and is offered to all sun deities.**

suffer both physically and mentally if we are deprived of natural daylight. When we talk of having a place in the sun, we are describing an enviable position where we can develop and grow, just as plants flourish in the sunlight.

Deities of the sun

In most traditions, the sun is associated with the male principle, though in archaic times it was perceived as an aspect of the great mother goddess. One example of a surviving female sun deity is the beautiful sun goddess of Shintoism, Amaterasu-o-mi-kami, ruler of the high plains of heaven, who wove the fabric of the universe in her sacred weaving hall. The Arunta people of Australia recount the myth of the sun woman Yhi. Germanic and Norse tribes revered Sunna, and the Celtic sun goddess

Light a gold candle on your sun altar first thing in the morning, as part of your ritual for greeting the day, and to honour whichever sun god you have chosen as your focus.

CATS IN THE SUN

The Egyptian goddess Bastet, the daughter of Re, was first worshipped as a solar deity who represented the sun's life-giving warmth. After about 1000 BC she was portrayed with the head of a cat, perhaps because of that animal's fondness for basking in sunshine. Bastet was generally a benevolent and protective goddess of love and fertility, and cats were venerated in her name.

The whole cat family is identified with the sun and the element of fire. Michael, the angel of the sun, can be called upon if a cat is in need of help. If you have a cat, you may notice it responding to the energy of your altar, and sleeping there.

Sul was adopted by the Romans, who dedicated altars over the sacred spring at Bath to Sulis Minerva.

In patriarchal societies, the sun became a male deity. Re, the Egyptian sun god, was revered as the creator of the world, whose tears engendered humanity. The Egyptians believed that Re would one day tire of his creation and return the world to chaos; therefore he had to be placated by their worship to safeguard the future of the cosmos. But they also looked to him for fatherly protection, and his regular daily progress across the sky was evidence of the celestial order that kept them safe.

The rayed sun-disc is an important symbol in many religions, and is related to the wheel of existence. For Zoroastrians, the winged sun-disc is the manifestation of Ahura Mazda, the supreme embodiment of light and goodness. In Christian imagery, a halo of golden rays surrounds the heads of the blessed, and Jesus is described as the 'light of the world'. In the Roman Empire, Jesus inherited the role of Mithras, god of light and emblem of invincible resurrection.

Solar symbols

An altar dedicated to the blessings of light and the fiery energy of the sun needs to stand in the southern quarter of a room. Dress it with the colours of sunlight: a sparkling golden cloth, orange and yellow flowers and citrus fruits. Sunday is the day of the sun, and the ideal time for a special ritual is on this day, at noon, when the sun is at its zenith. Kneel in front of your altar, raise your arms in a salute to the sun at the height of its cycle and draw in its energy and power. This is a time for vigour and self-reliance, and for fostering creative energy.

On every day of the week, light a gold or orange candle each morning to represent the light of the divine presence, and make offerings of saffron, turmeric and rosemary. You may choose to call on the power of a sun deity: Apollo for creativity and harmony, or Vishnu, the protector of the world. Or ask for the intercession of the Archangel Michael, the prince of the sun.

▷ To invoke the power of the sun into yourself is to draw in the light of life.

Combining the elements for success

We seek to achieve success in all the different areas of our lives. While fire is the element that will inspire you with the passion, energy and creativity that spur you on to great things, it can also be helpful to bring aspects of the other elements to your altar, to give expression to the finer distinctions of your aims and desires.

Creative success

Invoke the element of fire with glowing reds and oranges to inspire you with creative energy. If you feel that your progress in a creative sphere has been blocked, call on the transformative power of fire to release your spirit.

Place objects on your altar that represent your unachieved dreams: with this act you are enshrining your desire for self-expression. Instead of remaining an unavowed wish, your creative intent is brought out into the open and becomes a conscious goal. This acknowledgement will give you the impetus to turn your dream into reality.

▽ Add touches of violet and yellow to your altar to inspire you with new ideas.

Academic achievement

To help you achieve success in examinations and tests, you could add to your altar the colours and symbols of air, such as a yellow cloth and two yellow candles. Add feathers and images of birds to help your mind take flight. The fresh influence of air will inspire you with original thoughts and enhance your analytical powers. Air is also the element of new beginnings, so if a new opportunity presents itself to you, air will help you to succeed in it.

Success at home

The home is the centre of family life, and the arena of relationships and emotional issues. For success in these areas, incorporate the element of water in your achievement altar, representing it with the colour blue and with sea shells, sea creatures and water plants.

The sea is governed by the cycles of the moon, and its ebbing and flowing tides are reflected in the cycles of women's bodies, so water is related to fertility. Use the altar

△ Write a list of obstacles to your success, and burn the paper in the flame of a black candle.

▽ A simple arrangement of feathers helps your mind to take flight and achieve new heights.

▷ These tiger lilies' vibrant colours act as a fire symbol and will also evoke a tiger's strength.

BELTANE

The Celtic fire festival of Beltane ('bright fire') at the beginning of May celebrates the increasing light and heat of the returning summer. It is an appropriate time to perform a ceremony to aid fertility of any kind: for conceiving a child, increasing energy or helping a business to prosper. Traditionally, couples who wanted a child would leap the Beltane bonfire, symbolically taking the flame of life into themselves.

Hawthorn or May blossom is the traditional decoration at this time, for the altar and the rest of the house. It is usually considered unlucky to bring the blossom indoors, but the taboo is lifted on May Eve.

to help you visualize your pregnancy if you wish to conceive, and, if this seems difficult for whatever reason, to give you faith and hope to achieve.

Removing obstacles

A ceremony at your altar can also empower you to remove obstacles that you feel are blocking your path and preventing forward movement and growth. While you meditate on your wishes for yourself, think about all the things that could be holding you back and write them down. Expressing your

problems in writing in this way may help you to see them in a fresh perspective.

Place a single black candle on your altar between the two coloured candles, as black is the colour of banishing and release. Standing before the altar, light the black candle and burn the paper in its flame. As it burns, visualize each obstacle being transformed in the flame and carried away on the rising smoke.

▽ For an altar dedicated to successful family life, add water symbols to represent the emotions.

Altars of Water

In the realm of the subconscious, dreams and emotions ebb and flow, exerting their subtle influences on our conscious thoughts. Invoke the fluid power of the water element on any altar dedicated to love and relationships.

The element of water

Water is the element of love and the emotions, because it is as fluid as our feelings. It rules friendship and marriage. It also relates to the subconscious mind, constantly shifting and active beneath the surface, and this element therefore governs intuition. It influences sleep and dreaming, as we sink down into the swirling depths of the subconscious to discover our deepest desires.

The moon tugs at the oceans of the world to create the tides, which follow her

▽ **The moon is the ruler of the water element, creating the tides and influencing human moods.**

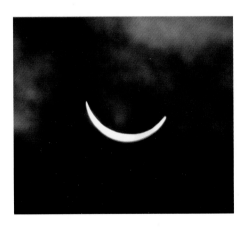

ever-changing cycle. She exerts the same pull on the fluids in our bodies, affecting our emotions, menstrual cycles and health. Thus the ebb and flow of water is mirrored in the cycles of our own lives.

The energy of water is feminine and receptive. It rules the west, the direction of the setting sun. Water is an element of purification and healing: this can take the form of healing counsel leading to emotional release, sweeping away stale feelings and inducing us to face the truth about ourselves. People dominated by water are sensitive and spiritual. It is cleansing and essential to life, and our own lives begin in water. The element is thus symbolized by the womb and is related to fertility.

Areas of the home ruled by water are the bathroom and the kitchen sink. Because it presides over friendship and relationships, it also governs the living room, the arena of social interaction. In its cleansing and healing role water is also the element of medical rooms and hospitals. In the natural world its places are seas, lakes, rivers, marshes, pools, wells and rain-drenched lands.

△ **Water may be cleansing and soothing, but it also possesses frightening, unstoppable power.**

▽ **Though fluid and changeable, water has the power to overcome obstacles in its path. Over time it carves its way through the hardest rock.**

◁ **Like ripples on a calm pond, our moods and emotions spread out to affect those around us.**

Neptune, the Roman god of the sea, was revered by seafarers whom he generally protected, but they feared his temper: his mood could change in an instant, giving rise to perilous ocean storms. Venus, the archetype of love and beauty, was said to have been created from the foam of the sea, and to have been carried on a sea shell to Cyprus. As she stepped from the sea, drops of water that fell from her body turned into pearls at her feet. The goddess had the power to calm the sea and ensure safe voyages, just as she could bring balance and harmony to human instincts and emotions.

Epona was a Celtic horse goddess worshipped during the period of the Roman Empire. She was portrayed carrying fruit or corn to show her connection with fertility and the earth's abundance. She was also a goddess of water and healing, and was the presiding deity of healing springs.

Invoke these deities to bless an altar with the energy of water.

WATER CORRESPONDENCES

DIRECTION: west.
SEASON: autumn.
TIME: dusk.
MOON PHASE: full.
PLANETS: moon, Neptune, Venus.
GENDER: feminine.
COLOURS: blue and orange.
SENSE: taste.
MAGICAL TOOLS: chalice, cauldron, mirror.
INSTRUMENTS: cymbals and bells.
CREATURES: cat, frog, turtle, dolphin, whale, otter, seal, fish.
NATURAL SYMBOLS: shells, water, river plants, watercress.
TREES: willow, alder, ash.
HERBS: chamomile, hops, lemon balm, orris, seaweeds, yarrow.
INCENSE: jasmine, rose.
MINERALS: silver, copper, amethyst, aquamarine, turquoise, tourmaline, opal, jade, pearl, sapphire, moonstone.
SIGNS: Cancer, Scorpio, Pisces.
ARCHANGEL: Gabriel.

Gods and goddesses of water

Deities associated with water are Tiamat, Venus, Neptune and Epona. Tiamat represents chaos and the raw energy of the salt ocean. In Mesopotamian mythology, she was the primeval mother whose waters mingled with the fresh water of Apsu to initiate the creation of the gods.

▽ **The dolphin is an animal of the water element, and symbolizes understanding and awareness.**

A family altar

Creating an altar in your home places it in the heart of your family, and will have an uplifting effect on everyone. Use it to celebrate and deepen the bonds between you. You might invite all the members of the family to help you make the altar, each bringing an object to it that symbolizes an aspect of themselves.

You can use photographs of your loved ones to bring spontaneity and humanity to the altar and to act as a focus for your prayers and thoughts about your family. To honour your relationship with your partner, choose a happy and harmonious picture of the two of you together. Other items could include gifts to you from your children, especially presents or drawings made by them, which will bring with them fond memories and the resonance of the love that motivated the gift.

Include objects that represent family members as they are now – acknowledging your children as turbulent teenagers, not just as enchanting toddlers, for example – so that the altar grows with the family and remains relevant. If pet animals are part of your family, remember to include reminders of them on the altar too.

◁ **Paint a protective rune on a stone and place it beside the photograph of someone who needs it.**

Altar placement

If you have an old piece of furniture that has been handed down to you through the generations, this could be the perfect site for an altar dedicated to your family. It will carry the blessings of those it served in the past. To observe feng shui principles, use the *pa gua* to find the area of your home that corresponds to the family. Or place your altar in the west where the water element governs relationships.

Incorporate blue crystals to aid communication: blue lace agate helps you express feelings, turquoise fosters partnership, light blue angel stone heals anger and lapis lazuli aids in the release of emotional wounds. Rose quartz is the stone of love.

If someone close to you is having problems in their relationships with others, either with friends or at work, surround a picture of them with rose quartz crystals for harmony. While you do this, think about the

△ **Place pictures and gifts from children in the family on the altar, to chart the passing of time.**

FLOWERS AND HERBS FOR HARMONIOUS RELATIONSHIPS

APPLE BLOSSOM: love, friendship.
CLOVER: fidelity.
COLTSFOOT: peace and tranquillity.
CYCLAMEN: love and truth.
GARDENIA: peace and healing.
HYACINTH: love and protection.
JASMINE: friendship.
LAVENDER: peace and happiness.
LILY OF THE VALLEY: peace, harmony and love.
NARCISSUS: harmony.
PASSION FLOWER: peace and friendship.
ROSE: love.
SWEET PEA: friendship and courage.
VERVAIN: inner strength and peace.
VIOLET: contentment.

▷ **If two family members are in conflict, put their pictures close together on your altar.**

person close to you and imagine them at ease with themselves and others. When someone leaves home, or begins a journey, write a protective blessing and tuck the folded paper into the frame of their picture.

Honouring older generations

In cultures with an established tradition of family altars, the ancestors are the most honoured family members. Photographs and mementos of your forebears keep those you loved as a positive influence in your life, and provide a sense of continuity for your children, helping them to see themselves as links in a continuous chain of existence.

In Spanish-speaking countries – particularly Mexico – the Day of the Dead is one of the most important religious occasions of the year. Families have picnics in the cemeteries and build altars covered with flowers and food to welcome their dead relatives home for the night, burning candles and copal incense to help them find their way. The dead are entertained as respected members of the family.

▽ **To help communication between members of your family, use blue stones on the altar.**

▽ **If someone in the family needs special love and care, surround their picture with rose quartz.**

An altar for healing

The home altar can be a source of healing for physical, emotional or spiritual problems. If you are in need of healing, call on the divine spirit to help you focus healing energies on yourself. Seek the wisdom to listen to your body and work in harmony with it to restore it to wholeness. If another person who is dear to you is suffering in some way, ask for help on their behalf.

Enlist the aid of the cleansing energy of water by setting an altar for healing in the west, and stand facing west to make your offerings or to say prayers. Make the altar a vision of pure watery beauty, fresh with the colour blue and decorated with flowers such as jasmine, lilies, lotus, iris or poppies, or with water-smoothed pebbles, shells, seaweed or watercress. Choose sandalwood incense, which is associated with purification and healing, or the cool, cleansing scents of camphor or eucalyptus.

If someone is receiving treatment in hospital, a small altar can be very comforting. You can simply arrange a blue shawl or scarf on a windowsill or side table, where it can be seen easily from the bed. Place on it images of wholeness and health, perhaps with some beautiful white flowers or other natural forms that speak of the vibrancy of the world that waits outside to be enjoyed.

A healing ceremony will be most effective during the time of a waning moon – particularly in the four days following the full moon. This is the time when things can be cast away or released, including grief and anger. To perform a healing ceremony on behalf of someone who is ill, light two blue candles on the altar and present a bowl of clear spring water as an offering.

Ask for the healing help of Archangel Gabriel, or Ceridwen, the white goddess of the Celts, or appeal to the compassion of

△ **Write the names of people to whom you wish to send healing on the petals of white flowers.**

▽ **Set up a healing altar by someone's bedside to offer solace and beauty when spirits are low.**

▷ When you are sending healing thoughts, holding a quartz crystal helps to channel them.

HEALING CRYSTALS

AMBER: relieves depression.

AMETHYST: protects against weakness of the immune system, calms fear and defeats insomnia.

AVENTURINE: soothes the emotions and promotes balance and well being.

BLOODSTONE: calms in threatening situations; detoxifies the blood.

CARNELIAN: increases physical energy and power.

CHRYSOCOLLA: assists in the release of grief, worry and pain.

CHRYSOPRASE: helps to relieve tension and stress.

CLEAR QUARTZ: a powerful talisman for healing, known in many cultures as the 'all-healer'. It guards against loss of vitality and strength and draws out pain, raises self-esteem, balances emotions and increases insight.

GARNET: protects against depression; boosts sexuality and fertility.

HEMATITE: protects against negativity, may be helpful for jet lag.

JET: dispels irrational fear and guards against illness.

LABRADORITE: heals co-dependence and instils courage and clarity.

LODESTONE/MAGNETITE: balances the body, relieves the pain of arthritis.

MALACHITE: releases trauma, relieves depression, acts against negativity.

ROSE QUARTZ: comforts and heals, enhances cardiovascular health.

TOURMALINE: relieves stress.

Kuanyin, the Buddhist goddess of mercy. Using a silver pen, write the name of the person and their ailment on white paper or white flower petals, and float them on the water. Place a clear quartz crystal in the water, and hold a second crystal in your hands while voicing your prayer, so that it transmits the healing power. Visualize the ailment being lifted out of the sufferer and give thanks for their recovery.

THE GODDESS OF COMPASSION

Chinese worshippers flock to the shrines of Kuanyin to seek her favour, because they believe she can cure almost every sickness and alleviate every distress. Her image stands on many family altars in the East.

Kuanyin's name means 'One who sees and hears the cries of the whole world'. She carries a vial containing the dew of compassion, and cures the seriously ill by sprinkling a few drops on their heads. While the birthdays of the gods are usually celebrated with firecrackers to ward off evil, there are no explosions for Kuanyin because she is so pure that no evil would dare approach her.

◁ Place a quartz crystal in a bowl of water and hold another while you are sending your prayers: the crystal will transmit the healing.

A lunar altar

The moon presides over the deep mysteries of our inner world, and is especially the guardian of women. As the appearance of the moon changes from crescent, full and waning to dark, it exerts its gravitational force on the waters of the earth, creating the tides and affecting the pattern of the weather. We, who are creatures of water, are also subject to its sway. The moon has always been an object of wonder.

In the moon's periodic growth and decay, the ancients saw an echo of the seasonal patterns of their lives. As it seemed to be reborn each month, the moon was widely believed to be the abode of human souls awaiting rebirth. But while the sun, rising each morning without fail, represented the stability of the cosmos, the moon appeared changeable and dangerous. It ruled the weather and could raise floods and storms,

PHASES OF MOON MAGIC

NEW/CRESCENT MOON (days 1–2): new opportunities, health and personal growth.

1st quarter

WAXING PHASE (days 1–7, active time, days 3–7): expansion, development and motivation; associated with Artemis.

2nd quarter

HALF TO FULL MOON (days 8–14, active time, days 12–14): fertility, abundance, illumination; associated with Isis, Selene, Arianrhod.

3rd quarter

WANING PHASE (days 15–21, active time, days 15–18): release, insight, wisdom, healing; associated with Hecate, Angel Gabriel.

4th quarter

DARK PHASE (days 22–29/30): meditation and preparation, time of no action; associated with Hecate, Cybele, Ceridwen.

but it also brought life-giving rain: it was both creative and destructive, and lunar deities shared this duality. The Mayan goddess Ixchel, for instance, was a vengeful goddess of storms, but also a protector of women in childbirth.

Phases of the moon

Each phase of the moon's cycle came to be personified distinctly, as aspects of the 'triple goddess' or 'great mother' – maiden, mother and crone (or wise elder). The Greeks, for example, worshipped Artemis as the new moon, Selene as the full moon and Hecate as the waning and dark moon. These archetypal figures have appeared in the pantheons

△ Use lunar gemstones, clear crystals and lunar images to dedicate your altar to the moon.

▷ Blue and orange are the colours of the water element, ruled by the moon.

▷ Your lunar altar will help you to connect with the energy of moon deities, as you light a candle in their honour.

LUNAR GODDESSES

ARIANRHOD: the Celtic mother goddess and keeper of the silver wheel of stars, symbolizing time and fate.

ARTEMIS: the Greek goddess of the waxing moon and of wild places, defender of women; invoked by women in childbirth. Her Roman equivalent is Diana.

CERIDWEN: the Welsh mother, moon and grain goddess whose cauldron contains a potion for the gifts of inspiration and knowledge.

SELENE: the Greek goddess of the full moon, who rides in a chariot pulled by two white horses and presides over magic. Her Roman equivalent is Luna.

HECATE: the powerful three-headed Greek goddess of the waning moon, who rules magic, sorcery, death and the underworld.

ISIS: the Egyptian mother goddess, who governs magic, fertility and regeneration.

SOPHIA: the female representation of the holy spirit who stands for divine knowledge and wisdom.

CYBELE: the Phrygian dark moon goddess who governs nature, wild beasts and dark magic.

of many cultures, as their characteristics have been adapted and absorbed.

Although the Gregorian calendar is based on solar time, older calendars are calculated according to lunar cycles, and the moon determines the dates of many major religious festivals. The lunar cycle is celebrated by pagans at ceremonies known as 'full moon esbats', which celebrate the Goddess in all her forms.

Lunar ceremonies

The full moon is the time for ceremonies to 'draw down the moon', connecting with the energy of the deity to empower wishes and ask for blessings for others. Write your wishes for them with a silver pen and burn them in a candle flame.

Setting up an altar to the full moon can help with emotional balance, bringing peace and harmony in your relationships. Decorate the altar with a light blue cloth and images of the moon or her deities. Use silver or light blue candles, jasmine, lilies or water-loving flowers, and burn jasmine or sandalwood incense. Moonstones, pearls, aquamarine and clear crystals are all associated with the moon, and will help to focus lunar energy on your altar.

TOTEM ANIMALS OF THE MOON

BEAR: sacred to Diana, goddess of the new moon, and connected with dreams, meditation and intuition.

CAT: associated with the night and the lunar goddess Artemis, it represents the mystery of the moon.

COW: sacred to Isis, who is crowned with her horns; milk is considered to be one of the gifts of the moon.

FROG: brings cleansing rain and is also a lunar fertility symbol.

HARE: represents the cycles of the moon and is associated with fertility. Indian and Chinese myths tell of the 'hare in the moon' and Eostre, the Anglo-Saxon goddess of fertility, was depicted with the head of a hare.

OWL: considered to be a harbinger of death, it is associated with the wisdom of Hecate, goddess of the dark moon. Its hooting is most often heard when the moon is full during the winter months.

WOLF: bays at the full moon, and stands for the psychic aspects of moon wisdom.

Altars of the Earth

Stability, loyalty and reliability are the qualities of
the earth element, keeping us grounded and secure
in loving families and comfortable homes. Altars
dedicated to earth energy attract physical comfort
and prosperity, and help us to acquire the wisdom
of experience.

The element of earth

Earth is the element of all physical and material things, and its energy is grounding. It is our nurturing mother, and is related to health and prosperity. It is the densest of all the elements, whether it is represented by hard rock or fertile, moist soil, and it stands for stability. It is the solid foundation over which the other elements move.

People in whom the earth element is dominant are home-loving, dependable and loyal, and happiest when surrounded by their family. Earth's energy is receptive. It teaches patience and self-sufficiency, and helps us to recognize and accept our own characters – both their limitations and their potential. It shows us how to take responsibility for our lives and our destiny. Its symbol is the wise elder.

Earth's season is winter and its direction is north, where in the winter darkness the shifting, moving waters are frozen into immobility. In the natural environment, earth's place is a cave, the primal symbol of

△ **The immobility of ice represents the earth element, whose season is winter.**

▽ **Earth is the stable foundation under our feet, but it can also be massive and awe-inspiring.**

shelter. The cave's womb-like image makes it a symbol of birth and rebirth, where oracles speak and enlightenment is achieved. Forests, valleys and fields are other places of the earth element. In the home, earth governs areas of physical needs – the dining room and loo – and practical tasks: the workshop, greenhouse and garden. It is the element of buildings and their construction, and presides over financial institutions.

Earth is the element of ceremony and ritual, through which we regain our connection with the spiritual wisdom of nature. It shows us the way home.

Earth gods and goddesses

Some of the deities associated with earth are Gaia, Pan and the Horned God.

Gaia is the ancient Greek earth goddess whose name has been given in modern times to the life force of the earth. The daughter of Chaos, she gave birth to Uranus, the sky, and Pontus, the sea. Her

EARTH CORRESPONDENCES

DIRECTION: north.
SEASON: winter.
TIME: midnight.
MOON PHASE: dark.
PLANETS: Earth, Saturn.
GENDER: Feminine.
COLOURS: citrine, brown, black,
olive green, sometimes white.
SENSE: touch.
MAGICAL TOOL: pentacle.
INSTRUMENTS: percussion.
CREATURES: ox, dog, wolf, goat,
stag.
NATURAL SYMBOLS: fossils, stones,
grains and seeds, salt, earth.
TREES: cypress, pine.
HERBS: pennyroyal, lovage, sage.
INCENSE: myrrh, patchouli.
MINERALS: lead, emerald,
aventurine, pyrites, coal, onyx.
SIGNS: Taurus, Virgo, Capricorn.
ARCHANGEL: Auriel.

▽ **The wolf is a creature of the earth element,
and represents loyalty and family ties.**

△ **Earth's energy is fertile and abundant, seen in
the growth of all living things.**

union with Uranus produced the Titans, or giants, including Cronos (Time), the father of Zeus. Gaia was the pre-eminent prophetess, the first deity of the great oracle at Delphi. Even the other immortals were subject to her law. The Greeks worshipped her as the giver of dreams and the nourisher of plants and children.

In Greek mythology Pan was a shepherd, and his name is believed to be derived from a word meaning 'pasture'. He was easygoing, lazy, sensual and unpredictable, and represents the spirit of untamed nature. He was usually said to be the son of Hermes, and was portrayed with the hind legs and horns of a goat (one of the first animals to be domesticated). Pan was a very ancient god of wild things, and his importance gradually increased until he came to be worshipped as the 'Great God', and father of all living things.

The pagan Horned God, who is related to the Celtic fertility deity Cernunnos, represents sexuality and vitality. He is the consort of the Triple Goddess. Like Pan, he is represented as half-man, half-animal. As lord of the woods he is the hunter, but he is also identified with the hunted or sacrificial animal.

Invoke these deities to bless an altar with the energy of earth.

THE PENTACLE

This five-pointed star may be created from clay, wood, wax or metal. It is a protective symbol of positive power (represented by a circle which often encloses it). The five points represent air, fire, water, earth and spirit.

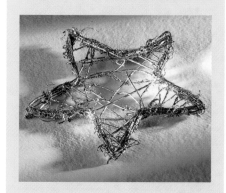

An altar for abundance

The laden altar of the harvest festival is a traditional manifestation of abundance. Corn, bread, fruits and vegetables are brought to the altar as offerings – to give thanks for the bounty of nature – but the mass of produce also acts as a visual re-assurance to members of the community: a reminder of both natural abundance and of their own abilities to harness earth's energy when they grow their food. The sight is an enriching one, expanding hearts and minds: it helps everyone to concentrate on all the good things they have, putting aside thoughts of what they lack.

Dedicating an altar to abundance is about tuning in to the blessings of life, shifting emphasis away from personal limitations and all that we lack, and opening ourselves to new and prosperous possibilities. Prosperity is not only a matter of material possessions, but an attitude of mind that includes spiritual and emotional riches. The altar can be

INCENSE FOR PROSPERITY

1 part cassia bark or cinnamon
1 part grated nutmeg
1 part finely grated orange rind
1 part star anise
Few drops orange essential oil
2 parts frankincense grains

Pound the first four ingredients using a pestle and mortar, bind with the oil and mix in the frankincense grains. Burn on a charcoal block.

a manifestation of that attitude and also a focus for meditations that build up inner abundance – the greatest wealth of all.

Use warm earthy colours such as russet, deep yellow, rich browns and olive greens. Add spicy scents to warm your soul and attract prosperity, such as patchouli, star anise, clove and cinnamon – or make up some prosperity incense mix. Make an offering of some silver coins. Think of all the things that already enrich your life and represent them on the altar to create a positive reminder of your spiritual wealth, and to express your gratitude. The more thankful you are, the more you will find greater abundance being drawn into your life.

The goddess of prosperity

An appropriate deity for this altar would be the Hindu goddess Lakshmi, who is the personification of abundance, wealth and

△ **An altar of abundance dedicated to Lakshmi, should reflect earth colours and scents.**

harmony. Deepavali, which is the third day of Diwali, the festival of lights, is dedicated to her worship: lamps are lit inside every home to welcome her and fireworks are exploded in her honour.

Lakshmi is portrayed as a beautiful woman seated on a sacred lotus throne. With two of her four hands she offers blessings of love and joy, while gold coins fall from the other two into the ocean of life. She is a symbol of everything that is fortunate, and it is the nature of good fortune that it is distributed randomly. But the elephant-headed god Ganesha, the lord of obstacles, helps to clear the path of anything that stands in the way of good fortune, therefore his presence on the altar can also help to bring abundance into your home.

◁ One of the best ways to find abundance is to have gratitude for everything you receive.

CHAI SHEN, THE GOD OF WEALTH

Chinese families have for generations set up an altar outside their homes on the eve of the Lunar New Year to receive the blessings of Chai Shen, the god of wealth, for the coming year. The god arrives from a different direction each year and this must be carefully calculated in case the altar is wrongly placed and welcomes the god of evil instead.

All the family members say prayers and make offerings that symbolize abundance and good fortune, including sweets, fruit and wine. Everyone writes their wishes for the year on red paper, which is burned with offerings of incense. Last year's portrait of Chai Shen is burnt and firecrackers are set off. After the ceremony, the god's portrait is carried inside to watch over the household for the next year.

▽ Be careful what level of prosperity you wish for – greed will not be rewarded.

A prosperity box

To focus on what you want to bring into your life, choose a box to be your 'prosperity box'. Using black ink, write a list of what you wish for. Then write another list using energy-enhancing orange ink: this list should contain all the things you are prepared to do in order to achieve your desires. Fold the pieces of paper and place both lists in the prosperity box, together with a handful of prosperity incense, a few silver coins and a small piece of jade to attract prosperity. Keep the box on your altar. When you receive a gift, leave that too on the altar for a while and always remember to give thanks for what you have, to sustain the flow of abundant energy.

▷ Prosperity boxes can also be filled with wishes for others and with offerings to the wish-granting powers you are calling upon.

An altar for grounding energy

The earth element is the solid ground beneath our feet. It is the stable foundation on which we rest, and it is earth's energy that allows us to live in the here and now, balanced and centred. Spiritual practices such as meditation and prayer may sometimes leave us feeling 'spaced out', dizzy, forgetful, or otherwise disconnected from daily life: tapping into the energy of earth brings us safely back to physical reality.

We can hold on to a strong connection with the earth by spending plenty of time outdoors, in a natural environment or in the garden. Gardening is a wonderful way to absorb earth energy, because it combines physical activity with the sensual pleasures of handling and working the soil, smelling the green scents of growing plants and hearing the natural sounds around us. Indoors, tasks such as cooking and cleaning are equally grounding. Music and art help to engage the senses. Sports, exercise and relaxation, which celebrate the body, help to increase our awareness of our physical reality, as do eating and drinking.

An altar to focus grounding energy needs to be visually evocative of the dark, weighty force of the earth. You could bring the outside into your home and use wooden elements, and earth offerings of soil, rice, leaves and stones, or choose a dark green or brown altar cloth and include pine cones, a bowl of sand, or salt. Salt, regarded as sacred in some cultures, is a product of the earth that is a powerful instrument of cleansing and preservation. Stones also help to

ESSENTIAL OILS WITH A GROUNDING EFFECT

Cedarwood
Patchouli
Pine
Rosewood
Sandalwood
Vetiver

suggest grounding energy, and dark crystals such as jet and smoky quartz are particularly associated with the earth element.

The pentacle symbolizes foundation and is used in ritual to represent the material world. It acts as a focus for energy and is sometimes used to ground stray energy in a room, or to channel energy into an object placed at its centre. Traditionally, materials taken from the earth help to reinforce the connection of the five-pointed star with the natural world – it is usually inscribed on a disc of wood, metal, or clay.

Select a number of small, smooth stones that appeal to you to form a pentacle shape on your altar and pour a pile of salt in the centre to focus earth's energy. Choose a dark crystal for a grounding ceremony; black or dark-coloured stones are also helpful for gaining resilience, quiet power and freedom from anxiety. Set the crystal in the salt to empower it with earth energy. Place a green candle at each point of the pentacle, and light them as part of your grounding ritual.

△ **Bring the outside into your home with an altar that will reconnect you with the earth.**

▽ **The five-pointed star, or pentacle, is a powerful symbol and can be used to channel energy.**

◁ A grounding visualization is helpful whenever you feel unconnected to reality, or to the natural world. It will also help to focus, stabilize and renew your positive energies.

CRYSTALS FOR GROUNDING

BLACK ONYX: protection against negative energy, good for emotional stability; encourages connection to material goals and their achievement.
BLACK TOURMALINE: grounding and protective, absorbs negativity.
HEMATITE: banishes fuzziness and aids concentration, memory and self-discipline; self-healing.
JET: grounding, earth power; wards off nightmares and avoids ill-health.
OBSIDIAN: very powerful grounding crystal, reduces escapism and dissolves anger and fear; snowflake obsidian has a softer effect, restores balance and clarity.
SMOKY QUARTZ: lightly grounding and balancing, counteracts hyperactivity, fosters self-acceptance and awareness of divine protection.

Grounding visualization

You can perform a grounding visualization using the pentacle altar, or simply sitting in front of a green candle set on a wooden base to represent the earth. Sit on the floor so that you are in physical contact with the earth, or sit on a chair with your feet on the ground. You will also need a dark crystal. Light each of the candles around the pentacle, or the single green candle in front of you. Take the crystal in both hands.

Breathing slowly and deeply, concentrate on the roots of a tree gradually growing down into the earth. Think of the strength of numerous small roots, locking themselves into the fertile soil, anchoring the tree firmly and working silently down towards the earth's core. Use these images to help you connect with the earth. Concentrate on your out-breaths and with each one feel the energy flowing downward through your body into the ground. Become aware of the constant, sustaining strength that lies beneath you, supporting you.

As earth's strength brings you comfort and confidence, bring its energy back into you by concentrating on each in-breath. Picture the green energy flowing up through the roots of the tree into the trunk and branches, and visualize this power flowing into you, until you feel calm and centred. Release the crystal and place it on the altar, then say a prayer of thanks and snuff out the candles. Remember to cleanse your crystal after the visualization.

◁ Salt is the best material to clean a dark crystal after a grounding session.

An altar for exploring wisdom

The inner journey is a quest for understanding and insight. Regardless of how much is known or learnt, no information can be of true benefit until we have understood how to make the best use of it, and this ability is defined as wisdom. It is an alignment of thought, feeling and experience, and it is only in the light of life experiences that we acquire it.

Wisdom is represented in the person of the sage, or wise elder – someone who has lived long enough to gain experience. If a child or young person seems wise, it is said that they are 'old before their time'. Yet we accrue wisdom throughout life, gaining insight through periods of reflection in solitude and with other people, when experience can be pooled and we can benefit from the learning processes, achievements and errors of others. With wisdom, we can apply knowledge to make sound decisions.

A vast body of traditional 'wisdom literature' has been handed down by ancient sages who spent their lives pondering the eternal truths of life and humanity's place

△ Juno Lucina, the light-bearer, is an ideal deity to invoke for wisdom and illumination.

▽ **Sage placed in a shell increases a connection with the Goddess, to whom shells are sacred.**

in the universe. In the Judaeo-Christian tradition, for example, these revered texts include many books making up the Bible, Islam is embodied in the Koran, as revealed to the Prophet Muhammed. Hindu wisdom is set out in the Upanishads and the Bhagavadgita, while Buddhists study the Sutras to learn the teachings of Gautama Buddha, and Taoists find wisdom in the Tao Teh Ching and the I Ching. Classical texts of wisdom include the works of Aristotle and Plato.

Aristotle defined two aspects of wisdom. The first concerns the meaning of life – the 'big picture' – which can be sought through meditation and spiritual practices. The second is a more practical kind of wisdom

SOPHIA

In the Hellenistic, Jewish and early Christian traditions, Sophia (the Greek word for 'wisdom') was acknowledged as the female aspect of the divine, and the eternal mother of all. According to the Gnostics, Sophia was born from silence before the beginning of creation. Her greatest shrine was the church of Hagia Sophia, built in Constantinople during the 6th century.

▷ Touch each sage leaf to the candle flame and then drop it into a heatproof bowl to burn and release its sanctifying smoke.

which might almost be described as common sense: the ability to look at things afresh to find ways around everyday problems. In both respects, our exploration of wisdom can lead to a greater perception and acceptance of the connectedness of all things, and an awareness that this wholeness or integrity – the order of the cosmos – includes ourselves. By learning detachment from the individual and particular, we rise above the concept of a separate self to reach a higher level of consciousness that is at one with the universe.

Wisdom can lead us along the right course in our individual lives, but even more important is its role in the wider world, where only the integrating vision of true wisdom can move society towards a more equitable state.

An altar to the Goddess

In the iconography of the Triple Goddess, the third manifestation of the deity is the crone, or wise elder. Her wisdom stems from long experience and she is associated with old age, the closing of the year and the evening of the day, when thoughts turn inwards to memories of the past and visions of the future. She is personified as Hecate

or Cybele, deities of the waning and dark moon, which is the time when insights can be gained. In the darkness of the winter night, the images of the mind's eye lead towards enlightenment.

To evoke the wisdom of the Goddess, dress an altar in purple, the priestly colour of inspiration and spiritual strength. An inspirational figure for its centrepiece could be the Goddess herself, or an image of a wise man or woman whose vision you particularly respect. A figure of an animal that represents an aspect of earth's wisdom could act as an ally in your quest for insight. Focus your thoughts with an amethyst, which brings spiritual peace and good judgement, and aids meditation.

Burn white sage in your ceremony at the altar. Sacred to the Romans, sage was also

used in native American shamanic rites to cleanse and sanctify, and is known as 'grandfather sage' because it represents wisdom. It clears the head and promotes insight. Hold each sage leaf in the flame of a violet candle before dropping it into a shell or bowl to burn, and let its cleansing smoke awaken your wisdom.

◁ Think of the wisest grandparent figure you can imagine when you burn sage, and allow its fragrance to permeate your mind.

ANIMAL TOTEMS

BEAR: going within to find wisdom.
CAT: intuition.
JAGUAR: focused power.
OWL: inner wisdom, vision, the unconscious.
RAVEN: mystery, secrets, memory and thought.
TORTOISE: ancient wisdom, experience, endurance.
WHITE BUFFALO: generosity, selflessness, spirituality.

An altar for divination

The altar is a place of prayer and hope: it may enshrine and honour aspects of the past, but it also looks forward to the future. In its traditional role as a place of sacrifice and offering, it is set up to win the attention of the gods and gain their favour in order to achieve peace, happiness and fulfilment in the future.

Spiritual practices such as prayer look forward to a hoped-for future, and visualizations and affirmations are attempts to carry the force of the present into the future – to achieve the kind of future we desire. These kinds of vision have a self-fulfilling power to help us achieve our goals. Projecting ourselves into a future existence of our imagination can help us to decide whether we really want to take a particular path in life, or whether we are being channelled by outside forces. Looking into the future helps to increase our self-awareness.

The future is an unknown land that we long to explore, and those who claim to possess psychic gifts or oracular powers have been both honoured and feared throughout history. But to some extent we all have visions of the future, for if we did not look ahead we would never be able to move forward. Time-honoured methods of divination, using aids such as the runes or the Tarot, help us tune into our intuition and point us in the right direction. Divination can be as simple, however, as sitting before your altar and gazing into the flame of a candle. As you do so, concentrate on channelling your thought processes in a way that releases your intuitive abilities to find the right direction.

Scrying

From the earliest times, individuals have seen images in shiny surfaces such as a pool of dark water, a black stone, a concave mirror or a crystal ball set against black velvet. In Tibet, seers sometimes gaze at a wetted thumb nail. The process is called 'scrying', which means 'perceiving', and it is a way of answering questions about the future.

There must be no distracting reflections on the surface of the object (known as the speculum), so the light on the altar should be soft and shaded. If a vision is to emerge, the mind and body need to be stilled and

◁ As you look at the candle flame let your eyes soften and your mind open up to itself.

▽ If you wish to see visions, place a crystal ball on your altar, or gaze at the images of the Tarot.

▷ Take note of any thoughts, emotions or feelings that arise as you look into the crystal.

△ Shuffle the cards well and be open to the image of the card that offers itself, allowing it to convey its message to your soul.

calmed by a period of quiet contemplation, with the eyes closed so that residual images fade from the retina. Gazing into the speculum induces a trance-like state and allows ideas to emerge from the unconscious mind, as they do in dreams. The first impression may be of a mist, which eventually darkens and resolves into colours, shapes, symbols or complete images. Like the images seen in dreams, these are likely to relate to deep-seated issues and offer information that the conscious mind does not have access to. They may seem inexplicable at first, but become relevant later.

Divining with cards

The Tarot is a deck of 78 cards whose illustrations draw on numerology, astrology and other ancient forms of symbolism. The 22 cards of the Major Arcana (*arcana* means 'secrets') are generally agreed to portray the soul's journey through life in a series of allegorical scenes, and in many modern packs

the 56 cards of the Minor Arcana are also illustrated with scenes. Tarot divination has become highly developed and complex, particularly over the last century, but one way to use the cards is to meditate at your altar on the image of a single card.

Shuffle the cards while concentrating on a question to which you need an answer, such as 'What do I need in order to grow?' or 'How can I best fulfil my destiny?' or perhaps 'What limitations must I release in order to be successful and/or happy?' Cut the pack, take out the card that you have revealed and lay it on the altar. Meditate on the image you have chosen.

Do not look up the interpretation of the particular card in a book at first, but stay with the vibrations of the card. The image is likely to represent something you need to change, adopt or integrate into your life in order to progress. This kind of contemplation can help you to interpret images you have seen in a crystal ball.

INTERPRETING VISIONS

Visions in a crystal ball can only be interpreted by the individual who sees them, but like the symbols perceived in dreams, they sometimes seem to represent archetypes that have universal significance. Some visions are simply a mist of colour.

WHITE: good fortune.

YELLOW: obstacles to come.

ORANGE: troubled emotions, anger.

RED: danger.

BLUE: business success.

GREEN: health and happiness.

GREY/DARK: misfortune.

RISING CLOUDS: affirmative.

SINKING CLOUDS: negative.

FAR-OFF VISIONS: the distant past or the future.

FOREGROUND VISIONS: the present or near future.

An altar for endings

Just as modern life has tended to lay aside the traditional rituals marking the beginnings of new stages of life, it also increasingly ignores endings. A ceremony to honour the completion of a cycle releases those involved to begin on a new enterprise.

By dedicating an altar to a part of your life that has ended, you are allowing yourself time and space to come to terms with the change you have had to make. You can also use an altar of remembrance to commemorate friends who have moved far away, or even to help you re-establish once-valuable relationships that for some reason have disappeared from your life.

Memorial shrines

Setting up an altar in the name of someone dear to you who has died gives you the opportunity to come to terms with your loss over time. Photographs and mementos help you to remember them in life, and lighting a candle in their name honours their memory and registers your gratitude for your relationship with them. It's important to choose items that remind you of your whole relationship with them, not just of the end of their life.

When someone dies, the impulse to erect a shrine in their memory is universal. The memorial honours the dead among the living, and also acts as a focus for all the

△ To remember our forebears is to offer them acknowledgement for our existence and thanks for their gift to us of life.

THE END OF THE SUMMER
The pagan festival of Mabon marks the Autumn Equinox and acknowledges the time when darkness begins to reign over light at the beginning of winter. The passing summer is celebrated; thanks are given for the end of the harvest and the year's experiences are weighed up. It is a potent time for the completion of tasks and the ending of quarrels. As the sun begins to die the dead are honoured.

thoughts and emotions we still need to communicate to the person who is lost.

In many countries, beautiful and unusual shrines can often be seen beside the road, erected by families to remember those they have lost in traffic accidents. More spontaneous tributes of flowers, photographs, notes and candles, whether marking the site of a personal tragedy or a major disaster, also have a powerful spiritual force, and are a natural reaction to the traumatic events of modern life.

▷ Red's link with the planets Mars and Pluto will give strength in times of vulnerability.

Altars for severing ties

A special altar can mark retirement or the ending of a career, helping you to complete this phase of your life before moving on to a new one. The end of school or university is another significant completion, both for the graduate who is about to embark on independent life, and for his or her parents, who may be coming to terms with their child leaving home.

A different way to use an endings altar is to visualize a desired ending to something that you would prefer to leave your life. This might involve severing your ties with a job, a place or a person who is obstructing you, or it might signify your wish to end a period of conflict or illness. Symbolize the ties that you feel are binding you by using a ribbon in a ceremony that will help you release yourself.

For an altar to end conflict you will need to create a red altar, using a red cloth, red ribbons, a red candle and some coriander seeds and basil leaves. A blue altar will represent the ending of ill-health or emotional stress, and can also help to end emotional ties. Use a blue cloth, blue ribbons and a blue candle and add a piece of turquoise

▽ The colour blue is linked to the moon, the planet of healing and feeling.

and a sea shell. Amber can also be added to the blue altar. To end anxiety or mental stress you will need to use the colours yellow and white. Add citrine and topaz gemstones and white or lavender flowers.

When you have prepared your altar, perform a cutting ties ceremony. This is best done at the time of the waning moon, as this is the time to cast away grief and anger. Light a coloured candle to match the ribbon on the altar and write down the ending you desire on a piece of paper.

Fold up the paper and wrap it in the ribbon, then lay it on the altar, focusing your will throughout on your wishes for release. When you feel the paper has been fully charged with your wishes, take up the parcel and cut through the ribbon, visualizing the completion of the situation in the way you want. Burn the paper completely in the candle flame. Take the pieces of ribbon outside, bury them in the earth and leave them there undisturbed.

▷ Burning the paper you have written on in the flame of the candle will complete the endings ceremony and lead to a feeling of release.

Completion

Whenever you use the altar it is important to finish your ceremony in a gracious way that signifies completion. Formulate a few words of farewell – a blessing, an offering of thanks, or simply an amen – to take your leave of your sacred space. If you have to dismantle an altar, this also needs to be achieved with reverence. Take away each item with as much care as you used when placing it on the altar.

Correspondence charts

The symbolism of crystals

Amber: good luck stone, draws out disease and clears negativity and depression

Amethyst: peace, protection and spirituality; heals at all levels; releases from addiction, helps with meditation and peaceful sleep, eases transition between life and death

Angelite: heals anger, restores harmony, helpful in telepathic communication, connecting with angels and spirits

Aquamarine: helps in the expression of spiritual truths

Aventurine: healing at all levels, dissolves blockages, balances the emotions, green aventurine attracts good fortune and increases perception; pink aventurine heals relationships

Azurite: mental clarity and renewal, releases painful ideas from the subconscious

Beryl: enhances psychic ability

Black onyx: protects against negative energy, helps emotional stability, encourages connection with reality

Blue lace agate: symbolizes health and long life; grounding, brings inspiration and facilitates self-expression

Carnelian: aids creative flow, grounds in the present, inspires confidence, courage and motivation

Chrysocolla: soothes and calms, eases fear and guilt, attracts luck

Chrysoprase: emotionally uplifting, attracts abundance and success, spiritual energy

Citrine: prevents nightmares, enhances self-esteem and responsible use of power, brings abundance and material well-being

Clear quartz: amplifies energy, spiritually and emotionally healing and empowering, aids meditation

Diamond: symbolizes power, purity, strength, trust, commitment and love; instils wisdom and confidence

Emerald: physically healing and protective, lends insight and security in love

Garnet: stimulates energy, aids expression, strengthens love and friendship

Hematite: aids concentration, reasoning, memory and self-discipline; healing and protective

Herkimer diamond: releases energy blockages, helps with dream recall

Jade: clarity, justice and wisdom; balances the emotions, promotes peaceful sleep, attracts prosperity

Jet: lifts depression and wards off nightmares; brings wisdom, health and long life

Labradorite: develops psychic ability

Lapis lazuli: strengthens will, awareness, integrity in relationships; aids the release of emotional wounds

Malachite: healing, absorbs negativity, stimulates creativity and strengthens intuition

Moonstone: wishes, intuition and new beginnings; restores harmony in relationships, calms emotions and induces lucid dreaming

Moss agate: connects with earth spirits, brings abundance and self-confidence

Obsidian: protective and grounding, reduces escapism and dissolves anger and fear; snowflake obsidian has a softer effect, restores balance and clarity

Opal: visionary, attracts inspiration and insight

Pearl: enhances purity, clarity and grace

Peridot: warm and friendly, heals wounded self-esteem

Pyrites: harnesses creative thinking and practicality

Red jasper: connects with earth energy, emotionally calming

Rhodonite: fosters patience, selflessness

Rose quartz: heals emotional wounds, restores love of self and others

Ruby: amplifies emotions, releases and dissolves anger, attracts loyalty, awakens passion and beauty

Rutilated quartz: releases energy blockages

Sapphire: symbolizes peace, gives protection and prophetic wisdom

Smoky quartz: lightly grounding and balancing, counteracts hyperactivity, fosters self-acceptance and awareness of divine protection

Tiger's eye: creates order and harmony, stability, attracts beauty and abundance

Topaz: symbolizes light and warmth, heals and absorbs tension, attracts love and creativity

Tourmaline: grounding, healing and protective, absorbs negativity and brings discernment and vitality; green tourmaline attracts success; pink tourmaline induces peaceful sleep; watermelon tourmaline balances sexual energy; yellow tourmaline increases wisdom and understanding

Turquoise: symbolizes protection, blessing and partnership

Zircon: aids healing and sleep

The symbolism of plants and herbs

Angelica: burn dried leaves for protection and healing

Anise: keeps away nightmares

Apple blossom: for love and friendship

Basil: gives protection, repels negativity and brings wealth:

Bay: guardian of the house, protection against illness; burn leaves to induce visions

Bergamot: attracts success and prosperity

Blessed thistle: brings spiritual and financial blessings; fresh plant brings strengthening energy to a sickroom

Boneset: drives away evil

Cabbage: brings good luck

Catnip: encourages a psychic bond with cats, attracts luck and happiness

Chamomile: for meditation and relaxation; use in prosperity charms to draw money

Chickweed: for attracting love or maintaining a relationship

Chilli: assures fidelity and love

Cinnamon: aphrodisiac; draws money, protection and success

Clove: banishes hostile or negative forces and helps to gain what is sought; burn in incense to stop others gossiping

Clover: for love and fidelity

Coltsfoot: brings love, wealth and peace

Comfrey: for safety when travelling

Cyclamen: for love and truth

Dandelion: enhances dreams and prophetic power

Eucalyptus: healing and purifying

Fennel: protects from curses: hang round doors and windows

Gardenia: for peace and healing

Garlic: for magical healing, protection and exorcism; especially protective in new homes

Ginger: for success and empowerment

Grape: for fertility and garden magic, attracts money

Hibiscus: attracts love and aids divination and dreams

Honeysuckle: strengthens the memory, helps in letting go of the past

Hops: improves health and induces sleep

Hyacinth: for love and protection

Hyssop: purification; hang up in the home to dispel negativity

Jasmine: brings good fortune in love, friendship and wealth; raises self-esteem; induces lucid dreams

Juniper: calms and brings good health; berries are burned to ward off evil

Lavender: purifying; brings peace and happiness, love and sweet dreams

Lemon: attracts happiness, relieves stress

Lettuce: induces sleep, assists in divination

Lily of the valley: brings peace, harmony and love

Lime: increases energy, encourages loyalty

Lotus: emblem of enlightenment, elevates and protects

Magnolia: assures fidelity

Marigold: enhances visions and dreams, renews personal energy

Mistletoe: for protection, love and visionary ability; hang on the bedpost for beautiful dreams

Mugwort: for clairvoyance, scrying and dream interpretation

Mullein: gives courage, keeps away nightmares

Nettle: wards off curses, allays fear

Olive: brings peace of mind and fidelity in love, fruitfulness and security

Orange: attracts peace, power and luck

Orris: attracts love and romance

Passion flower: fosters friendship; brings peace and understanding

Pennyroyal: increases alertness and brainpower, brings peace between partners

Pine: grounding and cleansing, use for a fresh start

Rice: attracts fertility and money

Rose: blesses love, domestic peace, generosity and beauty

Rosemary: protects the home, brings mental clarity and sharpens memory; burn in incense to find the answer to a question

Sage: brings wisdom, fertility, healing and long life

St John's wort: burn leaves to cleanse and protect

Strawberry: for love and luck

Sweet pea: for friendship and courage

Thyme: for courage and confidence

Tuberose: for eroticism and romance

Valerian: brings love and harmony, keeps fighting couples together

Vervain: attracts money, protection, transforms enemies into friends

Vervain: for inner strength and peace

Violet: contentment and love

Willow: use leaves and bark for healing and to empower wishes

Gods and angels

Agni: Hindu god of fire

Amaterasu: Shinto sun goddess

Aphrodite: Greek goddess of love and beauty

Apollo: Greek god of the sun, medicine and music, patron of the Muses

Arianrhod: Celtic mother goddess and keeper of time and fate

Artemis: Greek goddess of the waxing moon, protector of women

Athene: Greek goddess of war, wisdom and the arts

Auriel: archangel, earth

Bastet: Egyptian goddess of love and fertility, represented with the head of a cat

Brigid: Celtic triple goddess, fire deity and patron of the hearth, healing, prophecy, inspiration and the smith's craft

Cassiel: angel who assists with overcoming obstacles

Ceres: Roman goddess of earth and agriculture

Ceridwen: Welsh mother, moon and grain goddess

Cernunnos: The Celtic horned god, like Pan he is a fertility god

Cybele: Phrygian dark moon goddess who governs nature, wild beasts and dark magic

Demeter: Greek goddess of the earth, corn and vegetation; represents abundance and unconditional love

Diana: Roman goddess of hunting and the moon; represents chastity and protects women in childbirth

Epona: Celtic horse-goddess of fertility, abundance and healing

Freya: Norse mother goddess of love, marriage and fertility

Gabriel: archangel of the moon, associated with the west

Gaia: primeval Greek earth deity, prophetess of Delphi, goddess of dreams

Ganesha: elephant-headed Hindu god of wisdom and literature, son of Parvati and Shiva, patron of business

Haniel: archangel of divine love and harmony, beauty and the creative arts

Hathor: Egyptian sky-deity, goddess of love, joy and dance, usually represented as a cow

Hecate: three-headed Greek goddess of the waning moon, who rules magic, sorcery, death and the underworld

Hermes: Greek messenger god; represents consciousness, transition and exchange

Hestia: Greek goddess of the hearth and stability

Indra: Hindu god of war; associated with weather and fertility

Ishtar: Mesopotamian goddess of sexual love, fertility and war

Isis: Egyptian mother-goddess, wife of

Osiris; represents life, loyalty, fertility and magic

Ixchel: Mayan goddess of storms and protector of women in childbirth

Janus: Roman guardian of the entrance and god of transition

Jizo: Japanese protector of children and travellers

Kali: destructive aspect of the Hindu mother-goddess

Kuanyin: Chinese goddess of compassion

Kwannon: Japanese goddess of compassion

Lakshmi: Hindu goddess of abundance, wealth and harmony

Lugh: Celtic sky-god, associated with skills and the arts

Luna: Roman goddess of the full moon

Maat: Egyptian goddess of truth, justice and order

Manjushri: Buddhist bodhisattva of wisdom

Mercury: Roman messenger god; associated with speech, breath, wind and magic

Michael: archangel of the sun, associated with rulership, marriage, music

Minerva: Roman goddess of wisdom

Mithras: Roman god of light

Nephthys: sister of Isis, the Egyptian mother-goddess, guardian of the dead Osiris

Neptune: Roman god of the sea

Osiris: Egyptian god of vegetation and judge of the dead, brother and husband of Isis; symbolizes regenerative power of nature

Pan: Greek horned god of wild things, half man, half animal

Parvati: Hindu mother-goddess, consort of Shiva

Raphael: archangel of the air element, associated with communication and business

Re: Egyptian sun god and creator

Sachiel: angel ruling justice and financial matters

Samael: protective archangel, helps with matters that require courage or perseverance

Sekhmet: Egyptian goddess represented as a lioness, the 'Eye' of Re and terrifying aspect of Hathor

Selene: Greek goddess of the full moon

Shang Ti: Chinese supreme god

Shiva: Hindu creator god, whose meditation sustains the world

Shu: Egyptian god of the air, creator of earth and sky

Sophia: divine knowledge and wisdom

Sul: Celtic sun goddess

Sunna: Norse sun goddess

Surya: Hindu sun god

Tara: Tibetan goddess of wisdom and compassion

Thoth: Egyptian god of wisdom and the moon, scribe of Osiris

Tiamat: Mesopotamian creator goddess

Tsao-chun: Taoist kitchen god

Uriel: archangel of high magic

Venus: Roman goddess of love and beauty

Vesta: Roman goddess of the hearth

Vishnu: Hindu protector of the world

Zeus: Greek supreme god

The symbolism of colours

Red: blood, passion, the life essence, power, physical energy, courage, bringing change in difficult circumstances. Associated with Mars, battle, the element of fire, the south, projective energy.

Pink: love and kindness, reconciliation, peace and harmony, compassion, gentle emotions. Associated with family, children and friendship, receptive energy.

Orange: abundance, fertility, health, joy, attraction, luck. Marks the boundary between the self and others. Associated with the sun, projective energy.

Yellow: communication, the intellect, learning, concentration, also movement, travel and change. Associated with Mercury, the element of air, the east, projective energy.

Green: the heart and emotions, love, also nature, gardens and growth, money and prosperity, employment. Associated with the earth element.

Blue: wisdom, patience, possibility, the healing of the spirit, idealism, truth and justice. Associated with the moon, the element of water, the west.

Purple: royal and priestly colour, a link with the higher dimension, wisdom, inspiration, magic, religion and spiritual strength. Associated with Osiris.

Violet: temperance, spirituality, repentance, transition from life to death.

Brown: earth and earth spirits, instinctive wisdom, the natural world. Practical and financial matters, the home, stability, old people, animals. A protective force.

Grey: compromise and adaptability, psychic protection and secrecy.

White: divinity, potential, the life-force, energy, purity. Contains

all other colours. Associated with the sun. Helpful for new beginnings, clear vision and originality.

Black: death and regeneration. Conclusions that lead to new beginnings, marking a boundary with the past, banishing and releasing negativity, shedding guilt and regret. Associated with Saturn, the Roman god of limitations, suffering and transformation.

Gold: worldly achievement, wealth, long life and ambition, confidence and understanding. Associated with solar deities.

Silver: dreams, visions, intuition, hidden potential. Associated with the moon and lunar deities.

Picture Acknowledgements

The publishers would like to thank these agencies for permission to use their images.

AKG:11tl, cave painting, paleolithic period, Combe d'Arc, Ardeche, France; 15b a *lararium* in a house, 1st century AD; 20br.

The Bridgeman Art Library: 10bl, Early Dynastic period, c2500BC, gypsum relief; 10tr, cave painting, paleolithic period, Cabrerets, France; 11b, entrance to megalithic cave, 3rd-2nd century, France; 12t, standing stone, 4th-3rd millenium BC, France; 13b, Stonehenge, Wilts, England; 14t, sacrificial ceremony from Pitsa, near Corinth, c530BC; 14b, libation of the dead, 16th century BC; 15t,

Roman altar, 1st century; 16b, Indra in Paradise, Gujarat, India; 17b, Buddhist shrine, Leeds Museums and Galleries UK; 20t, engraving, Fanny Parks, (after) 19th century; 20bl, *Faith*, 1912, Galileo Chini (1893-1956).

The Art Archive: 13t, Indian Shaman from George Catlin *Illustrations of the North American Indians*, 1876.

Sylvia Cordaiy Photo Library Ltd: 16t and 25tl, Julian Worker; 17tr Nick Smith; 18bl, David Lansdown; 19t, Moorcroft; 19b, K Harrison.

Christine Osborne Pictures: 23.

Mick Sharp: 21t; 22t; 24; 25tr; 25b.

Mirielle Vautier: 18t, 17tl.

Index